I Speak BASIC to My APPLE™

Aubrey B. Jones, Jr.

HAYDEN BOOK COMPANY, INC.
Rochelle Park, New Jersey

To Alyce, Aubrey III, and Adrienne

Library of Congress Cataloging in Publication Data

Jones, Aubrey B.
   I speak BASIC to my Apple™

Summary: An introduction to microcomputer and computer programming, with practice problems in writing simple computer programs, inputting the programs, and outputting the results.
1. Apple II (Computer)—Programming—Juvenile literature.
2. Basic (Computer program language) — Juvenile literature. [1. Apple II (Computer)   2. Basic (Computer program language) 3. Computers.   4. Programming (Electronic computers)]   I. Title.
QA76.8.A662J66   1982b   001.64'2   81-24436
ISBN 0-8104-6175-7   AACR2

Apple is a trademark of Apple Computer Co., Inc., and is not affiliated with Hayden Book Co., Inc.

Copyright © 1982 by HAYDEN BOOK COMPANY, INC. All rights reserved. No part of this book may be reprinted, or reproduced, or utilized in any form or by any electronic, mechanical, or other means, now known or hereafter invented, including photocopying and recording, or in any information storage and retrieval system, without permission in writing from the Publisher.

Printed in the United States of America

	10	PRINTING
83 84 85 86 87 88 89 90		YEAR

Contents

Part 1   **The Hardware (Or The "Boxes")** 1
Objectives; Typical Data Processing Operation; Basic Parts of a Computer; Summary; Practice 1

Part 2   **The Software ("The Program")** 17
Objectives; How Humans Talk to Computers; A BASIC Program; Apple II Keyboard; Apple II Power-Up Rules; Summary; Practice 2

Part 3   **Your First Computer Program** 39
Objectives; Writing Your First Computer Program; Executing Your Program; Expanding Your Program; Listing Your Program; Ending Your Program; Summary; Practices 3, 4, 5

Part 4   **More Programming Tools** 61
Objectives; Mathematical Operations; Programming Mathematical Operations; A BASIC Mathematical Program—Area of a Rectangle; Print Zones; Practices 6, 7

Part 5   **Scientific Notation** 82
Objectives; Scientific Notation; Review and Feedback; Practice 8

Part 6   **Relational Operators and IF-THEN/GOTO Statements** .. 89
Objectives; Relational Operators; Using IF-THEN Statements (Conditional Branching); Using GOTO Statements (Unconditional Branching); Practices 9, 10

Part 7   **Input Statements** 102
Objectives; Input Statements; Area of Rectangle Problem Revisited (Using Input Statements); String Variables; Practices 11, 12, 13

Part 8   **Using the Calculator Mode and Sizing Memory** 116
Objectives; Bit vs. Byte; How Much Memory Is Used in BASIC Programs; Summary; Practice 14

Part 9   **Using the Disk Drive** 125
Objectives; A Disk Drive as an Input/Output Device; Practices 15, 16, 17

Part 10   **Using FOR-NEXT-STEP Statements** 130
Objectives; FOR-NEXT Statements and Loops; Comparison of GOTO, IF-THEN, and FOR-NEXT Program Loops; Loop Flowcharts; Timer Loops; Practices 18, 19

Part 11   **Reading Data** 146
Objectives; READ-DATA Statements; Restore Function; Practice 20

Part 12	**Video Display Graphics**	**160**
	Objectives; Text Commands: TAB, HTAB, VTAB, NORMAL, INVERSE, FLASH; Graphic Commands: GR, COLOR, PLOT, HLIN, VLIN; Practice 21	
Part 13	**Arrays**	**187**
	Objectives; One-Dimensional Arrays; Two-Dimensional Arrays; DIM Statement; Summary; Practices 22, 23	
Part 14	**INT(X), ABS(X), and RND(X) Functions**	**202**
	Objectives; INT(X) Function; ABS(X) Function; RND(X) Function; Summary; Practices 24, 25	
Part 15	**Subroutines**	**216**
	Objectives; Subroutines; ON-GOTO; ON-GOSUB; Summary; Practices 26, 27	
	Extra Practices	**232**

PART 1

The Hardware (Or The "Boxes")

What You Will Learn

1. That the computer is a valuable tool that can solve problems, print words, draw pictures, store information, retrieve information, compare information, play games, and do many other things to help you in everyday life.

2. That people control computers and that computers cannot think (despite what you might have heard).

3. To identify and explain the basic parts of a computer and relate them to a "box diagram" of a general purpose computer.

4. To identify and explain the function of the basic parts of an Apple II microcomputer.

5. To define and explain the terms hardware, software, microcomputer, microprocessor, RAM, ROM, processor, input unit, output unit, memory, and binary.

6. That computers are simple and easy to use; and above all that computers are fun!

Welcome to the World of Computers!

People Control Computers!

Computers Can't Think!

Typical Data Processing Operation
"Box" Diagram

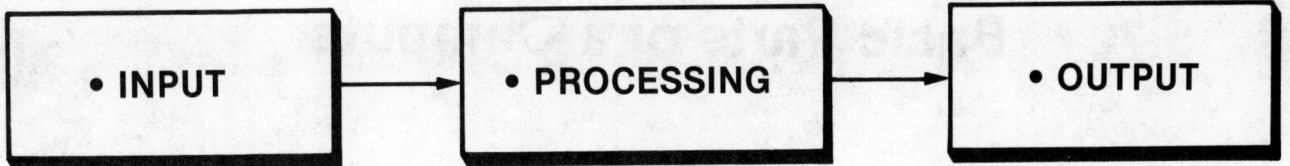

Examples of Data Processing Operation

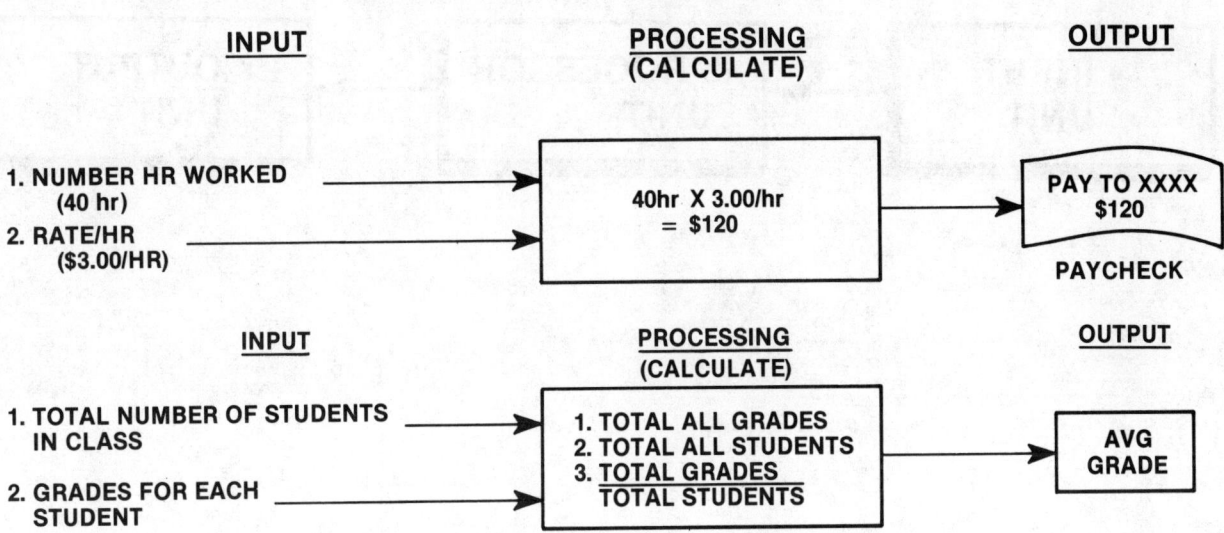

BOX Diagram
Showing
Basic Parts of a Computer

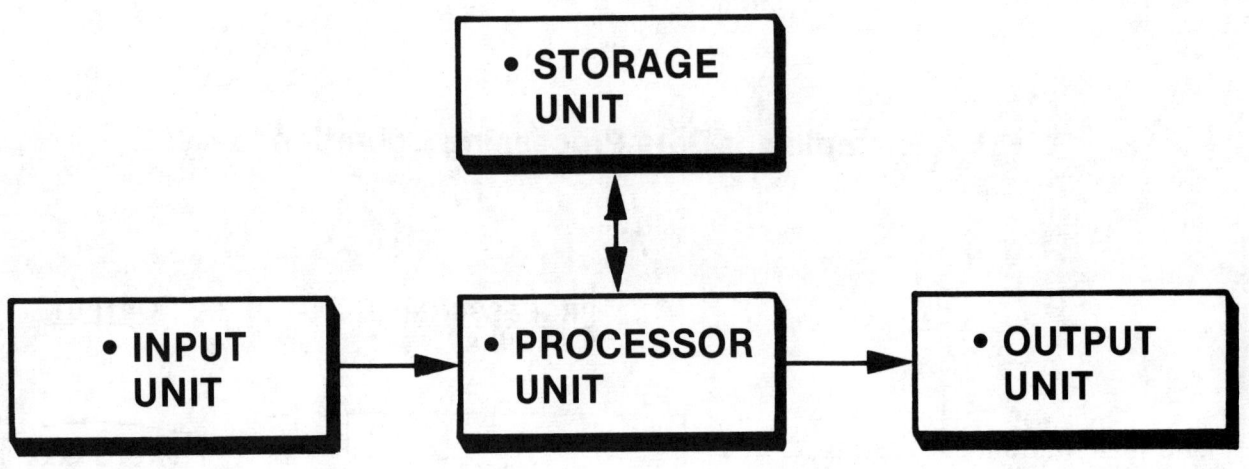

Stores or Remembers

- **Storage unit (memory)**
  - Stores both information and instructions until needed (requested)

Interprets, Controls, & Calculates

- **PROCESSOR UNIT**
  - **INTERPRETS (DECODES) INSTRUCTIONS AND REGULATES (CONTROLS) THEIR EXECUTION**
  - **PERFORMS ALL OF THE CALCULATIONS**

Box Diagram of a Basic Computer System

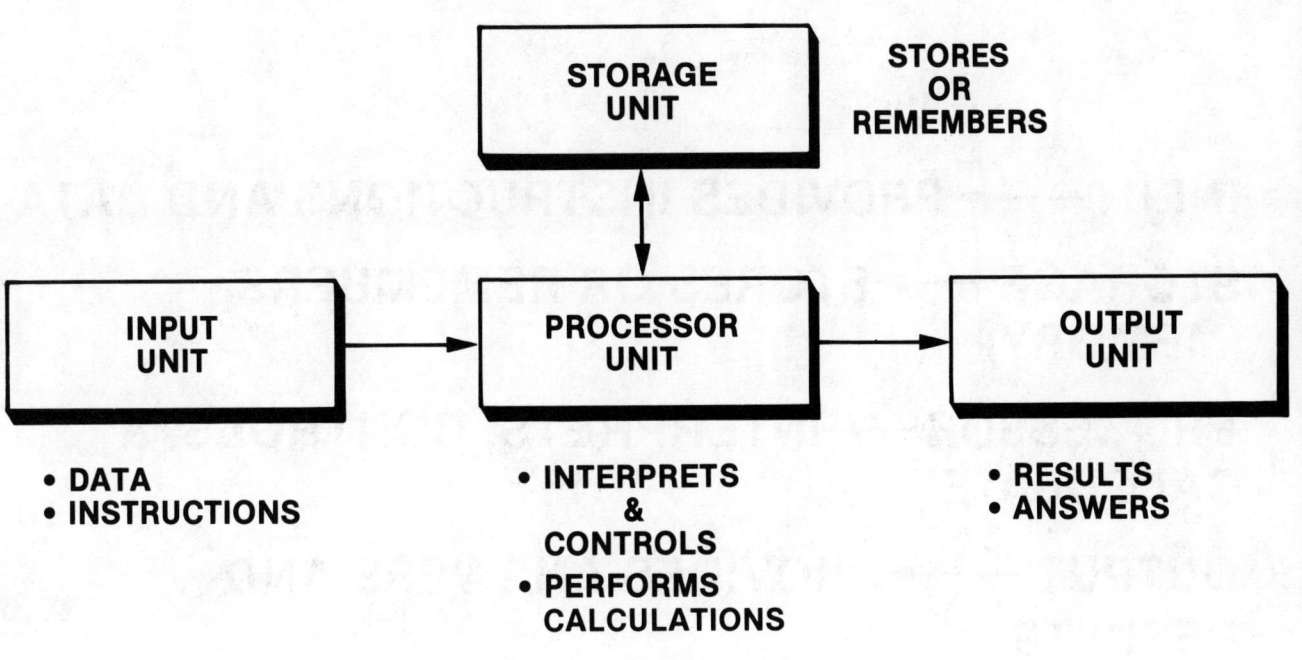

What We Have Learned

- INPUT ⟶ PROVIDES INSTRUCTIONS AND DATA
- STORAGE ⟶ STORES OR REMEMBERS
  (MEMORY)
- PROCESSOR ⟶ INTERPRETS, CONTROLS, & CALCULATES
- OUTPUT ⟶ PROVIDES ANSWERS AND RESULTS

Some Terms You Should Know

- **MICROPROCESSOR**
- **MICROCOMPUTER**
- **RAM**
- **ROM**

- **MICRO** = Very small

- **MICROPROCESSOR** = Very small processor

- **RAM** = Random access memory
  - **CAN BE** changed by the user
  - Information stored in RAM will be destroyed if power fails or is turned off (volatile)

- **ROM** = Read only memory
  - **CANNOT** be changed by the user
  - Information stored in ROM is not destroyed if power fails or is turned off (non-volatile)

  - Control program (BASIC interpreter) stored here

Box Diagram of a Microcomputer

- STORAGE UNIT
- INPUT UNIT
- MICROPROCESSOR UNIT
- OUTPUT UNIT

Basic Components of the Apple II Computer

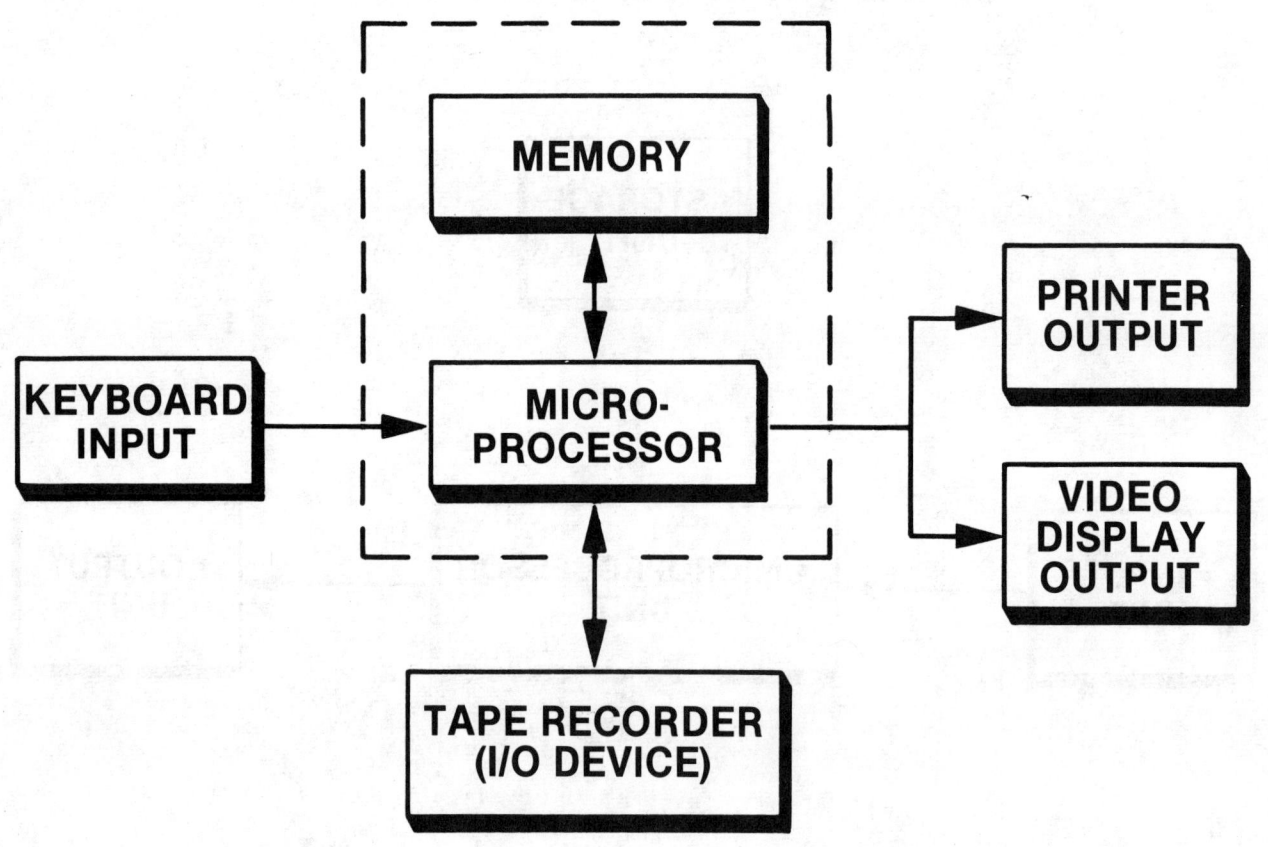

Courtesy of Apple Computer Company, Inc.

Courtesy of Apple Computer Company, Inc.

What We Have Learned

DATA PROCESSING OPERATION STEPS:	BASIC COMPUTER PARTS:	MICROCOMPUTER PARTS:
• INPUT ⟶	• INPUT UNIT ⟶	• INPUT UNIT
• PROCESSING ⟶	• PROCESSOR UNIT + MEMORY UNIT ⟶	• MICROPROCESSOR + MEMORY
• OUTPUT ⟶	• OUTPUT UNIT ⟶	• OUTPUT UNIT

PRACTICE 1

Box Diagram of a Computer

1. Draw the BOX DIAGRAM of a BASIC computer.
   a. Label each box with the correct name.
   b. List the functions of each box.

PART 2

The Software (The "Program")

What You Will Learn

1. To define the terms hardware, software, BASIC, binary, and interpreter, and to relate them to computers.

2. That computers speak a foreign language: machine language.

3. How humans talk to computers via a programming language called BASIC.

4. To identify the principal parts of a BASIC program.

5. To identify and explain the purpose of all the keys on the Apple II keyboard.

6. How to connect and power up an Apple II microcomputer.

Box Diagram of a Basic Computer System

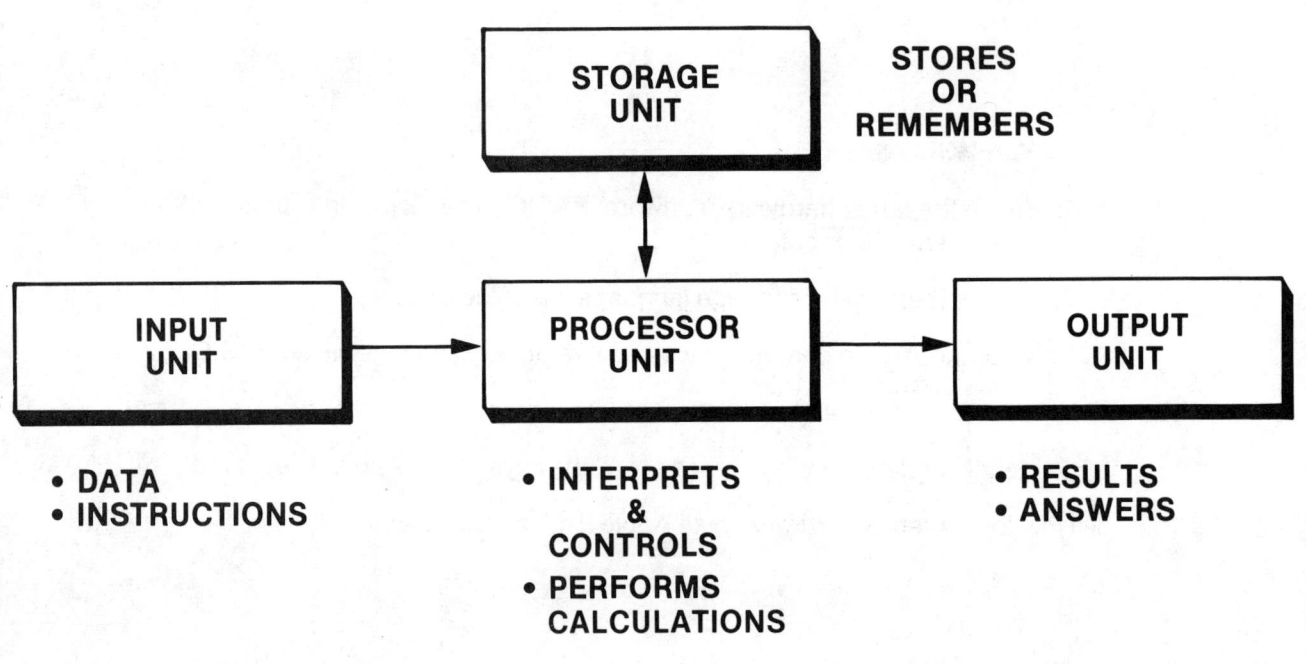

More Terms You Should Know

- **HARDWARE**
  - **— THE COMPUTER AND COMPUTER RELATED EQUIPMENT (THE BOXES)**

- **SOFTWARE**
  - **— THE INSTRUCTIONS FOR THE COMPUTER (THE PROGRAM)**

Computers Speak a Foreign Language!
(No Speak English, French, German Spanish, or Any Other Natural Language)

- **COMPUTERS SPEAK IN *MACHINE* LANGUAGE**

  — **MACHINE LANGUAGE IS A FORM OF *BINARY* CODING**

  — **BINARY IS A WORD DENOTING "TWO"**

  — **MACHINE LANGUAGE USES TWO BASIC SYMBOLS: "Ø" AND "1"**

How Humans Talk to Computers

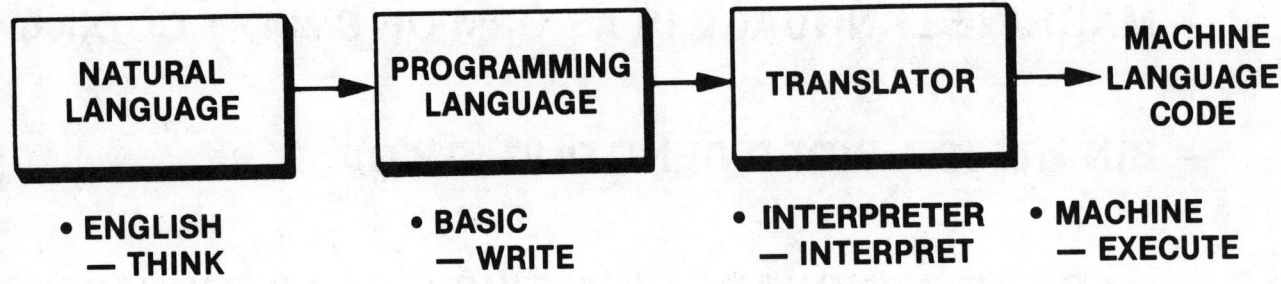

- **BASIC**

    (Beginner's all-purpose symbolic instruction code)

    — Popular programming language for writing instructions to the computer

- **INTERPRETER**

    — Translates BASIC into machine code
    — (You really don't have to know anything about an interpreter since it is used automatically when you run a BASIC program)
    — Located in the ROM in Apple II

To Program You Must Learn the Language First!

A Comparison between English and BASIC

ENGLISH LANGUAGE
- Words
  — Used to make sentences
- Sentences
  — Used to make paragraphs
- Paragraphs
  — Lengths vary
- Commands
  — Can be one word
  — e.g., STOP! HALT!
- Sentence Numbers
  — Optional (seldom used)

BASIC PROGRAMMING LANGUAGE
- Key Words
  — Used to make statements
- Statements
  — Used to make programs
- Programs
  — Lengths vary
- Commands
  — Executed immediately
  — e.g., NEW, LIST, RUN
- Line Numbers
  — Must be used for each statement

Learning a New Vocabulary

Here Are the Key Words and Commands You'll Learn:

KEY WORDS
- PRINT
- END
- LET
- INPUT
- GO TO
- IF --- THEN
- REM
- STOP
- FOR --- NEXT
- READ-DATA

COMMANDS
- NEW
- LIST
- RUN
- CONT

Commands vs. Statements

COMMANDS

— Executed as soon as you type them and press RETURN

STATEMENTS

— Put into programs and are only executed after you type the command RUN and press RETURN

A BASIC Program

	LINE NUMBER	KEY WORD	OTHER PART OF THE STATEMENT	"LOOK AT" REQUEST*
1st STATEMENT	1∅	PRINT	"HELLO THERE"	RETURN
2nd STATEMENT	2∅	PRINT	"YOUR NAME"	RETURN
3rd STATEMENT	3∅	END		RETURN
COMMAND	RUN			RETURN

*Pressing the RETURN key tells the computer to "LOOK AT" (and store) what you have just typed. You must press this key after each statement or command.

Line Numbers

— Serve as a guide to the computer in running the program.
— Tell the computer in what order it should carry out your instructions.
— Computer will start executing at lowest numbered line unless told to start elsewhere.
— Normally are multiples of 5's, 10's, or some other multiples to leave space for inserting new program lines between old one.
— Although it is perfectly legal to number program lines more closely (like 1, 2, 3, 4, etc.), don't do it!

Key Words

- Never used alone
- Need line number
- Always part of a BASIC statement that has some other part to it*
- Executed only after command RUN is typed and RETURN key is pressed

*To the purist, we know that key words like END and STOP can be used alone; but you still need line numbers, and you must type RUN and press RETURN to execute.

What We Have Learned

- **Key words**
  - Used to make statements
- **Statements**
  - Must have line numbers and key words
  - Used to make programs
- **Programs**
  - May vary in length
- **Commands**
  - Executed as soon as you type them and press RETURN

APPLE II KEYBOARD

Special Function Keys on the Apple II Keyboard

KEY   FUNCTION

CTRL
- Stands for "Control." Several keys have an additional function that is obtained by holding down the CTRL key while the other keys are pressed.
  - Control characters never appear on the display but the computer responds by performing certain actions.
  - For example, holding down the CTRL key and pressing G causes the computer to go "BEEP." (See other control key functions on next page.)

ESC
- Stands for "ESCAPE." Pressing ESC key puts the computer in the EDIT mode.
  - ESC unlike CTRL key does not have to be held down while typing another key. (Forget about EDIT mode for now.)

REPT
- Stands for "Repeat." Holding down the REPT key while pressing another key makes the other key's character appear repeatedly on the screen.
  - First, you must hold down the key for the character you wish repeated, then hold down the REPT key.

RESET
- Press this key if your Apple Computer does not respond correctly to your instructions. (If this does not work try turning your Apple off and on again. Of course, if you do this you will lose your program.)
  - If your Apple contains Autostart ROM, accidentally pressing the RESET key causes no problems because you are immediately returned to the BASIC you were just doing. However, with the Old Monitor ROM, accidentally pressing the RESET key will cause problems. (See page 148 of Applesoft Tutorial on how to recover from accidental resets.)

Special Function Keys on the Apple II Keyboard (cont'd)

KEY	FUNCTION
[RETURN]	• Causes the computer to "look at" line you just typed in and to act accordingly. This key must be pressed each time you want to enter a line from the keyboard. — [RETURN] also causes the cursor to "RETURN" to the screen's left edge.
[SHIFT]	• Some keys have two characters printed on them. This key permits you to type upper characters such as quotes ("). Hold down [SHIFT] key while typing key with two symbols if you want to type the upper symbol. — Once exception is the [BELL/G] key. Holding down the [SHIFT] key and typing [G] will *not* give you the "BELL." Use [CTRL] and [G] if you want the "BELL" to ring (BEEP). — Another exception: holding down [SHIFT] and typing [M] gives a right-hand square bracket (]), although a bracket symbol does not appear on the key.
[←] (Back space)	• Backspaces the cursor one space at a time. As the cursor moves, one character is erased from the program line which you are currently typing.
[→] (Retype)	• Moves the cursor to the right. As it does, each character it crosses on the screen is entered as though you had typed it. Therefore, it is called the "Retype" key.

Control (CTRL) Key Functions

KEY	FUNCTION
CTRL	• Stands for "CONTROL." Holding down this key while other keys are pressed causes the computer to perform different actions. Here are some examples:
CTRL B	— Pressing the RESET key first then holding down the CTRL key while typing B will put you in Applesoft BASIC instead of Monitor or Machine language program.
CTRL C	— Stops the computer. This will cause the prompt character (]) and the blinking cursor (■) to appear. To continue execution, type CONT and press RETURN.
CTRL G	— Causes the computer to "BEEP." CTRL G is called a "BELL" because the present keyboard design is based on the teletype where CONTROL G actually rings a bell.
CTRL S	— Stops a program listing. To restart the program listing, type CTRL S again. Unlike CTRL C, CTRL S will permit the listing to continue where it left off.
CTRL X	— Tells the computer to ignore the line currently being typed, without deleting any previous line of the same line number. A backslash (\) is displayed at the end of the line to be ignored.

Apple II Power-Up Rules (Autostart ROM)

ACTION	DISPLAY
1. Make certain system is connected properly. (This procedure assumes you are not using a disk.)	
2. If the tape recorder is connected, it should be in the *STOP* mode.	
3. Turn on the video display.	
4. Turn on the Apple. The switch is on the back of the computer next to where the power cord plugs in. Push this switch into the upward position.	
5. The display should appear as shown. → (The] is called the "prompt" character and the blinking square is called the "cursor".)	APPLE II]■
6. If your display does not look as shown in the description above, do the following:	
(a). Make sure the switch on the back of Applesoft firmware card is in the up position (See Applesoft reference manual for more details.)	
(b). If your Apple doesn't seem to respond correctly, a press of the RESET key will usually remedy the problem.	
(c). If pressing the RESET doesn't work, turning the Apple off and then turning it back on again will probably correct the problem.	

Apple II Power-Up Rules (Old Monitor ROM)

ACTION

1. If your Apple looks like this when you turn it on, it contains the Old Monitor ROM. To begin running BASIC after turning on your Apple, you must always go through the following sequence.
2. Press the [RESET] key (you should hear a "beep").
3. Hold down the [CTRL] key and continue to hold it down while you type the letter [B].
4. Press the [RETURN] key.
5. Type [HOME] and then press [RETURN] and your screen should appear as shown. →
6. The] indicates that the computer is now in the Applesoft BASIC Mode and ready for you to use.

DISPLAY

```
??@@??@@??@@??@@??@@??@@??@@??@@??@
??@@??@@??@@??@@??@@??@@??@@??@@??@
```
(Your screen displays a lot of random characters on the screen like shown above, plus an asterisk (*) in the lower left together with a flashing cursor (■).
*■

]■

Getting It Together

- **STEP 1 — WRITE YOUR PROGRAM**
- **STEP 2 — GET THE COMPUTER READY**
- **STEP 3 — ENTER YOUR BASIC PROGRAM**
- **STEP 4 — RUN YOUR PROGRAM**
- **STEP 5 — SIGN OFF**

PRACTICE 2

Becoming Familiar with the Apple II

Become familiar with the Apple II by doing the following (you should actually go through every step):
1. Power up (turn on) the Apple II using the power-up rules (see page 35).
2. How many power buttons did you have to press? _____
3. Where were the buttons located? _____
4. Where is the reset button located? _____
5. Where is the power indicator located? _____
6. Locate the [SHIFT] key.
   a. How many [SHIFT] keys are there on the keyboard? _____
   b. Hold down the [SHIFT] key and press every key that has a second character on the key (e.g. ! and #). What happened? _____
   c. What happened when you held down the [SHIFT] key and pressed [G]? _____
   d. Now hold down the [CTRL] key and press [G]. What happened? _____
7. Locate the [REPT] key.
   a. Hold down another key first ([B] for example) and then press [REPT]. What happened? _____
   b. Now try other keys with [REPT].
8. Locate the backspace [←] and retype [→] keys.
   a. Type HOME and press [RETURN] key. (This should clear the screen with the exception of the prompt character (]) and the blinking cursor (■).)
   b. Type the following (just as shown)
      ] PRINT "CAT"   ■
      ↑   ↑
      Prompt   blinking cursor
      What does the cursor do each time you type a character? _____
   c. Use the backspace [←] key to move the cursor over the C. Now change the "C" to a "B." Where does the cursor appear now? _____
   d. Press the [RETURN] key. What happened? _____
   e. Now retype the line PRINT CAT. Then backspace to the [C] and change the [C] to [B] again. But this time use the retype key to move the cursor to the end of the line. The line should look like this:
      ] PRINT "BAT" ■
              ↑
           cursor
   f. Now press [RETURN] key. What happened? _____
   g. Try additional examples until you feel comfortable. Use the backspace [←] and retype [→] keys.
9. Locate the [CTRL] and [ESC] keys. You will learn more about them later.

38

PART 3

Your First Computer Program

What You Will Learn

1. To enter and run your first BASIC program.

2. To explain the purpose and use of the following BASIC commands: LIST, NEW, RUN.

3. To explain the purpose and use of the following key words: PRINT, PRINT (for spacing), REM, END.

4. To explain the purpose and use of the following special function keys: CTRL, REPT, RETURN, SHIFT, ← (back space), →, (retype), RESET, ESC.

5. To explain the purpose and use of the following miscellaneous points:] prompt, ■ cursor, " " (quotes), line numbers, reset button, power-up rules.

Special Function Keys on the Apple II Keyboard (Review)

KEY	FUNCTION
CTRL	• Stands for "Control." Several keys have an additional function that is obtained by holding down the CTRL key while the other keys are pressed. — Control characters never appear on the display but the computer responds by performing certain actions. — For example, holding down the CTRL key and pressing G causes the computer to go "BEEP." (See other control key functions on next page.)
ESC	• Stands for "ESCAPE." Pressing ESC key puts the computer in the EDIT mode. — ESC unlike CTRL key does not have to be held down while typing another key. (Forget about EDIT mode for now.)
REPT	• Stands for "Repeat." Holding down the REPT key while pressing another key makes the other key's character appear repeatedly on the screen. — First, you must hold down the key for the character you wish repeated, then hold down the REPT key.
RESET	• Press this key if your Apple Computer does not respond correctly to your instructions. (If this does not work try turning your Apple on and off again. Of course, if you do this you will lose your program.) — If your Apple contains Autostart ROM, accidentally pressing the RESET key causes no problems because you are immediately returned to the BASIC you were just doing. However, with the Old Monitor ROM, accidentally pressing the RESET key will cause problems. (See page 148 of Applesoft Tutorial on how to recover from accidental resets.)

Special Function Keys on the Apple II Keyboard (Review) (cont'd)

KEY	FUNCTION
[RETURN]	• Causes the computer to "look at" line you just typed in and to act accordingly. This key must be pressed each time you want to enter a line from the keyboard. — [RETURN] also causes the cursor to "RETURN" to the screen's left edge.
[SHIFT]	• Some keys have two characters printed on them. This key permits you to type upper characters such as quotes ("). Hold down [SHIFT] key while typing key with two symbols if you want to type the upper symbol. — Once exception is the [BELL / G] key. Holding down the [SHIFT] key and typing [G] will *not* give you the "BELL." Use [CTRL] and [G] if you want the "BELL" to ring (BEEP). — Another exception: holding down [SHIFT] and typing [M] gives a right-hand square bracket (]), although a bracket symbol does not appear on the key.
[←] (Back space)	• Backspaces the cursor one space at a time. As the cursor moves, one character is erased from the program line which you are currently typing.
[→] (Retype)	• Moves the cursor to the right. As it does, each character it crosses on the screen is entered as though you had typed it. Therefore, it is called the "Retype" key.

Control (CTRL) Key Functions (Review)

KEY	FUNCTION
CTRL	• Stands for "CONTROL." Holding down this key while other keys are pressed causes the computer to perform different actions. Here are some examples:
CTRL B	— Pressing the RESET key first then holding down the CTRL key while typing B will put you in Applesoft BASIC instead of Monitor or Machine language program.
CTRL C	— Stops the computer. This will cause the prompt character (]) and the blinking cursor (■) to appear. To continue execution, type CONT and press RETURN.
CTRL G	— Causes the computer to "BEEP." CTRL G is called a "BELL" because the present keyboard design is based on the teletype where CONTROL G actually rings a bell.
CTRL S	— Stops a program listing. To restart the program listing, type CTRL S again. Unlike CTRL C, CTRL S will permit the listing to continue where it left off.
CTRL X	— Tells the computer to ignore the line currently being typed, without deleting any previous line of the same line number. A backslash (\) is displayed at the end of the line to be ignored.

Apple II Power-Up Rules (Autostart ROM) (Review)

ACTION	DISPLAY
1. Make certain system is connected properly. (This procedure assumes you are not using a disk.)	
2. If the tape recorder is connected, it should be in the *STOP* mode.	
3. Turn on the video display.	
4. Turn on the Apple. The switch is on the back of the computer next to where the power cord plugs in. Push this switch into the upward position.	
5. The display should appear as shown. → (The] is called the "prompt" character and the blinking square is called the "cursor".)	APPLE II]■
6. If your display does not look as shown in the description above, do the following:	
(a). Make sure the switch on the back of Applesoft firmware card is in the up position (See Applesoft reference manual for more details.)	
(b). If your Apple doesn't seem to respond correctly, a press of the RESET key will usually remedy the problem.	
(c). If pressing the RESET doesn't work, turning the Apple off and then turning it back on again will probably correct the problem.	

Apple II Power-Up Rules (Old Monitor ROM) (Review)

ACTION

1. If your Apple looks like this when you turn it on, it contains the Old Monitor ROM. To begin running BASIC after turning on your Apple, you must always go through the following sequence.
2. Press the RESET key (you should hear a "beep").
3. Hold down the CTRL key and continue to hold it down while you type the letter B.
4. Press the RETURN key.
5. Type HOME and then press RETURN and your screen should appear as shown. →
6. The] indicates that the computer is now in the Applesoft BASIC Mode and ready for you to use.

DISPLAY

??@@??@@??@@??@@??@@??@@??@@??@
??@@??@@??@@??@@??@@??@@??@@??@
(Your screen displays a lot of random characters on the screen like shown above, plus an asterisk (*) in the lower left together with a flashing cursor (■).
*■

]■

The Three Modes of Apple (Important to Remember)

- **This course is designed for using your Apple computer in the Applesoft BASIC. But you must be able to tell at all times which language or mode the computer is in. You can do this by simply looking at the prompt character. Here are the prompt characters you are likely to see:**

    * **Indicates that you are in the Monitor Program which advanced programmers use when working in "Machine Language."**

    > **Indicates that you are in Integer BASIC mode.**

    ] **Indicates that you are in Applesoft BASIC mode.**

Typical Display Readout

```
10      PRINT      "HELLO THERE"

20      PRINT      "YOUR NAME"

30      END

RUN
```

Writing Your First Computer Program

YOUR ACTION	DISPLAY

YOUR ACTION

1. Before you start typing your program, always type NEW and press the [RETURN] key.

2. Type the line exactly as shown: ⟶

3. Use [SHIFT] key to type the upper characters like the quotation marks (") and the exclamation point (!).

4. Do *not* press [RETURN] key yet!

5. Go back and examine your typed line *very carefully*. Did you make a mistake? If you did, just use the backspace [←] key to move the cursor over the incorrect character. (Note: If you made a mistake at the beginning of the line, you will have to move the cursor back to that point and then use the retype [→] key to move the cursor to the end of the line.

6. Is everything OK? If it is, you can press [RETURN]. (This tells the computer to "look at" what you just typed in).

7. The prompt] should appear. The computer is saying, "It's your turn ...I'm waiting for you."

DISPLAY

```
10 PRINT "HELLO THERE NAME!" ■
```
Ⓐ

```
10 PRINT "HELLO THERE NAME!"
]■
```

NOTE
Ⓐ Insert student's name
   Go to next page

Common Errors

- **Missing quotes (")**
- **Too many quotes**
- **Forgot the key word PRINT**
- **Forgot the line number**
- **Forgot to press RETURN**
- **Used the character "O" for the number "ZERO" (Ø).**
  (Note: A slash is used to help you to recognize a zero. Look at your keyboard closely.)

Writing Your First Computer Program — Almost? (Errors)

PROBLEM
(You Forgot to Follow Instructions)

1. **MISSING QUOTES (")** — You forgot to enclose everything after the word PRINT in quotation marks. (If you want something printed, don't forget the quotation marks!)

2. **TOO MANY QUOTATION MARKS** — You typed too many. (That won't work either!)

3. **FORGOT THE KEY WORD PRINT** — You forgot to type PRINT. (How will the computer know you want to print if you don't tell it to print?)

4. **FORGOT TO TYPE THE LINE NUMBER (10)** — Line numbers tell the computer where to start. The computer always starts executing from the lowest numbered line unless you tell it to start elsewhere. (We will show you how to tell the computer to start at another line later. Keep the faith!)

SOLUTION

- If you have already pressed RETURN, you must retype the entire line to correct your error. Here is how you do it:

- Type in the same line number you wish to change (10 in this case). That is, if you want the computer to replace that line with the corrected line.

- Next, retype the line exactly as shown on previous page. (But follow directions this time, Dummy!)

- Then, check line over for errors.

- If everything is OK, don't forget to press RETURN! When you press RETURN it tells the computer to "look at" what you just typed and to act accordingly.

Read this page if you had any errors! Then correct your errors before going to the next page!

Executing Your Program

YOUR ACTION | DISPLAY

1. Tell the computer to execute or run your program. The command for this is simple: RUN.
2. So type *RUN* and press RETURN .
3. If you made no mistakes, the display will read: ⟶ HELLO THERE NAME!
4. If it did not work, try again (i.e., check your program for errors).
5. If it did work, let out a yell, "HEY, I CAN DO IT TOO!"

Go to next page (if you completed this one OK)

Using the Retype Key to Save Time

YOUR ACTION

1. You typed Line 10 as shown but have *not* pressed RETURN (blinking cursor at the end of that line indicates you have not pressed RETURN).

2. You wish to change the "B" to a "D" or to PRINT AUDREY. So you use the backspace ← key to move the cursor to the left one space at a time.

3. Now type "D" but *don't* press RETURN yet. (Note that the cursor has moved to the next letter "R.")

4. Use the retype → key to move the cursor to the end of the line.

5. If you have finished typing the line and everything is correct, press RETURN. (Note that after you press RETURN the blinking cursor moved to the beginning of the next line.)

6. What do you think would have happened if you had pressed RETURN in step 3 above? (Your screen would appear as shown on the right. Do you know why?)

7. Remember you can always retype the entire line but the retype → key saves you time.

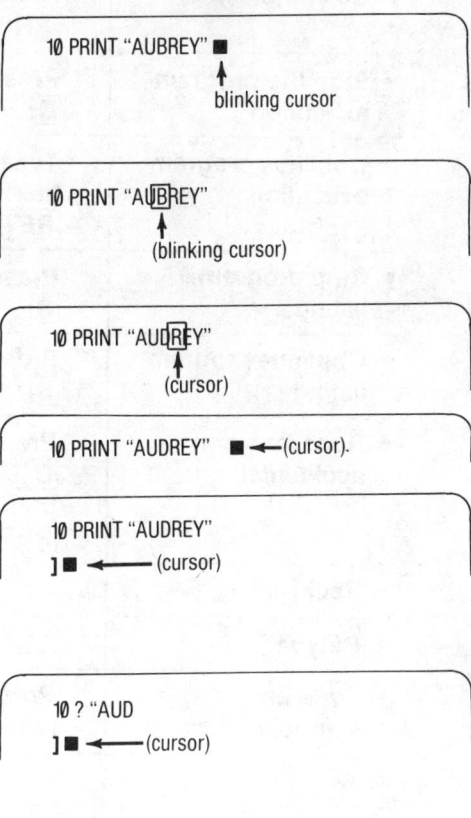

Some Helpful Keys and Commands to Remember

ACTION	KEY(S) TO PRESS	COMMAND
• Enter data	RETURN	—
• Clear the screen	Press ESC then SHIFT and P	HOME
• Stop the program execution	Press CTRL and C	STOP
• Continue program execution	Type C O N T, then press RETURN	CONT
• Stop program listing	Press CTRL and S	— (Applesoft Plus only)
• Continue program listing	Press CTRL and S	— (Applesoft Plus only)
• Recover from accidental RESET	Press CTRL and C then press RETURN	—
• Backspace	←	
• Retype	→	—
• Type upper symbol on key	Press SHIFT and desired key	—
• Reset	RESET	
• Enter Applesoft BASIC Mode (]) from Monitor Mode (*)	Press RESET then hold down CTRL, type B, and then press RETURN	—

Expanding Your Program

YOUR ACTION

1. You now have a program in the computer. (Unless you turned it off. If you did, retype line as shown):
2. Type in line 2Ø *exactly* as shown:
3. Check your new line (2Ø) *very carefully*, especially the quotation marks.
4. Everything OK? Press RETURN . (Remember, always press RETURN if you want the computer to look at what you typed.)
5. Let's run your program. Type RUN and press RETURN .
6. If you did it right, the screen will read:
7. If it did not work, check your program for errors.

   Go to next page

DISPLAY

```
1Ø PRINT "HELLO THERE NAME"

2Ø PRINT "I'M GOING TO MAKE YOU A SUPERSTAR!"
```

```
HELLO THERE NAME!
I'M GOING TO MAKE YOU A SUPERSTAR!
```

Using the PRINT Statement for Spacing

YOUR ACTION

1. Look at your video display. Would you like more space between the two lines? OK, this is how you do it.

2. Type in a new line as shown ⟶ and then press RETURN.

3. Now type *RUN* and press RETURN

4. WOW! A *PRINT* "nothing" puts a space between what you told the computer to print in Lines 1Ø and 2Ø.

5. Observe that the PRINT statement (Line 15) was placed between Lines 1Ø and 2Ø. Since you were smart enough to number your lines by 1Ø's, it was much easier to modify your program. (That's because you left room to insert new lines between the old ones.) Although it is perfectly legal to number program lines more closely (like 1, 2, 3, 4), don't do it.

   Go to next page

DISPLAY

```
HELLO THERE NAME!
I'M GOING TO MAKE YOU A SUPERSTAR!
```

```
15 PRINT
```

```
HELLO THERE NAME!

I'M GOING TO MAKE YOU A SUPERSTAR!
```

Inserting Remarks into a Program
(But Not Printing Them Out)

YOUR ACTION

DISPLAY

1. Another important key word is REM, which stands for remark. It is often convenient to insert remarks into a program. The main reason for inserting remarks is so you or someone else can refer to them later and know what the program is for and how it is used.

2. When you tell the computer to execute the program by typing RUN and pressing RETURN , it will skip right over any number line that begins with the key word REM. The REM statement will have no effect on the program. (Let's see about that!)

3. Type Line 5 exactly as shown and then press RETURN (*'s are just for decoration).

   ```
   5 REM *THIS IS MY FIRST COMPUTER PROGRAM*
   ```

4. Type RUN and press RETURN .

5. It is the same as before (REM statement was not printed).

   ```
   HELLO THERE NAME!
   I'M GOING TO MAKE YOU A SUPERSTAR!
   ```

   Go to next page

Listing Your Program
(Looking At Your Program to See What It Contains)

YOUR ACTION*	DISPLAY

1. To list your program is easy. The command is LIST.
2. Now you type LIST and press RETURN :

```
 5 REM * THIS IS MY FIRST COMPUTER PROGRAM*
1Ø PRINT "HELLO THERE NAME!"
15 PRINT
2Ø PRINT "I'M GOING TO MAKE YOU A SUPERSTAR"
```

3. You can call for a listing of your program any time the prompt] appears on the screen.

4. Also, you might only want to list one line. Type LIST 20 and press RETURN and the screen will display:

```
2Ø PRINT "I'M GOING TO MAKE YOU A SUPERSTAR"
```

5. You might also want to list several program lines, starting at one line and ending at another. For example, type List 1Ø - 2Ø and RETURN .

```
1Ø PRINT "HELLO THERE NAME!"
15 PRINT
2Ø PRINT "I'M GOING TO MAKE YOU A SUPERSTAR!"
```

*Type HOME and press RETURN so you can start with a clean display.

Go to next page

Ending Your Program

YOUR ACTION	DISPLAY

1. The end of a program is the last statement you want the computer to execute. Most computers require you to place an END statement after this point, so the computer will know it is finished. However, the Apple does *not* require an END statement. (Other computers might require it though.)

2. Let's add an END statement to your program. Type and enter: ⟶

3. Now type RUN and press [RETURN].

```
99 END

HELLO THERE NAME!

I'M GOING TO MAKE YOU A SUPERSTAR!
```

4. No change from before! The program ended, but it did not print "END."

5. Let's make it print THE END. (How do we do that?)

6. Oh, I remember! We need a PRINT statement. So let's try it. Type and enter: ⟶

```
98 PRINT "THE END"
```

7. Now *RUN* your program.

8. IT WORKED AGAIN! (If not, check the program.)

```
HELLO THERE NAME!

I'M GOING TO MAKE YOU A SUPERSTAR!
THE END
```

9. Note that there is no space between THE END and the line above it. Why? (Because you did not tell the computer to put a space between them!)

Learned in This Session

COMMANDS*	KEY WORDS**	MISCELLANEOUS	SPECIAL FUNCTION KEYS
• HOME	PRINT "MESSAGE"	] PROMPT	CTRL CONTROL
• LIST	PRINT (SPACE)	■ CURSOR	ESC ESCAPE
— LIST MM	REM	" " QUOTATION MARKS	RETURN
• NEW	END	LINE NUMBERING	SHIFT
• RUN		POWER (light)	← BACKSPACE
— RUN MM		• KEYBOARD LAYOUT	→ RETYPE
		• APPLE II POWER-UP RULES	REPT REPEAT
* Executed as soon as you type them and press RETURN	** Used to make statements. Statements are executed after you type RUN and press RETURN	• BEEP	RESET

NOTE: If you don't understand everything on this page, stop!
Go back over this session until you understand it thoroughly!
MM = Any line number (e. g., 10, 20, 30, etc.)

Assignment* 3-1

1. WRITE* A PROGRAM TO PRINT ON SEPARATE LINES
   A. Your Name
   B. Your Entire Address
   C. Your Telephone Number
2. EXPAND* YOUR PROGRAM TO INCLUDE THE FOLLOWING:
   A. Remark Statement to Describe Your Program
   B. Spacing between Each of the Lines Displayed (Printed)
   C. Include an End Statement
3. TYPE YOUR PROGRAM AND PRESS RETURN
4. RUN YOUR PROGRAM
5. LIST YOUR PROGRAM

* WRITE YOUR PROGRAM ON PAPER AND GET IT CHECKED BY YOUR TEACHER FIRST.

PRACTICE 3

Writing and Running Your First Program

1. Write a program to PRINT the following:
    a. Your name (first and last)
    b. Your school's name
    c. Your teacher's name
2. Enter and RUN it.

PRACTICE 4

Inserting Remarks and Spacing into Your Program

1. If you have erased the program from Practice 3, rewrite the program and do the following: (If you still have the program from Practice 3 in the computer, you do not have to rewrite the program.)
    a. Add a new program line with a remark statement to your program (any remarks you want to make).
    b. Have the computer insert one space between your name and your school's name in the output on the display (that is, you add the necessary program line).
    c. Have the computer insert two spaces between your school's name and your teacher's name in the output on the display.

PRACTICE 5

Listing and Ending Your Program

1. Rewrite the program from Practice 4 and do the following (Again, if you have the program in the computer, you don't have to rewrite it. But in case you don't know what is in the computer, just type NEW and rewrite the program.):
    a. Add an END statement to tell the computer it is the end of your program.
    b. Add a statement to have your computer PRINT "THE END."
    c. RUN your program.
2. List your program.
    a. How large is your program now? (How many lines?)
    b. Copy the program in your notebook.

PART 4

More Programming Tools

What You Will Learn

1. To enter and run more BASIC programs: mathematical programs, area of rectangle program.

2. To explain the order of mathematical operations using the M.D.A.S. rule.

3. To explain the purpose and use of the keyword: LET.

4. To explain the purpose and use of the BASIC mathematic operators: multiply (*), divide (/), add (+), subtract (−), exponentiate or raising a number to a power (∧).

5. To explain the function and use of commas, semicolons, and print zones.

6. To list and identify variables that can be used with Applesoft BASIC.

Review of Part 3

COMMANDS*	KEY WORDS**	MISCELLANEOUS	SPECIAL FUNCTION KEYS
• HOME	PRINT "MESSAGE"	] PROMPT	[CTRL] CONTROL
• LIST	PRINT (SPACE)	■ CURSOR	[ESC] ESCAPE
— LIST MM	REM	" " QUOTATION MARKS	[RETURN]
• NEW	END	LINE NUMBERING	[SHIFT]
• RUN		[POWER] (light)	← BACKSPACE
— RUN MM		• KEYBOARD LAYOUT	→ RETYPE
		• APPLE II POWER-UP RULES	[REPT] REPEAT
		• BEEP	[RESET]

* Executed as soon as you type them and press [RETURN]

** Used to make statements. Statements are executed after you type RUN and press [RETURN]

NOTE: If you don't understand everything on this page, stop! Go back over this session until you understand it thoroughly!

MM = Any line number (e. g., 10, 20, 30, etc.)

Math Operators

= (Equal)
+ (Add)
− (Subtract)
* (Multiply)
/ (Divide)
∧ (Exponentiation)

(∧) means raising a number to a power like 2^2, 2^3, or 2^4

Order of Arithmetic Operations

- **Multiply ⟶ Divide ⟶ Add ⟶ Subtract**
  (Left to Right)
  - "My Dear Aunt Sally"

- **If Parentheses are used**
  - Innermost level operations first
  - Then next level out
  - M.D.A.S. order inside parentheses

Order of Operations Example — (Without Parentheses)

- If there are no parentheses, the computer performs operations by going from left to right doing exponentiation operations (∧) first. Then (*) and (/) are done in order from left to right and finally (+) and (−) are done in order from left to right. (Remember M.D.A.S.!)

Example:

$$4 + 5 * 4 \wedge 3 - 4/2 =$$
$$4 + 5 * \boxed{64} \quad - 4/2 =$$
$$4 + \boxed{320} \quad - 4/2 =$$
$$4 + \quad 320 \quad - \boxed{2} =$$
$$\boxed{324} \quad\quad - 2 = \boxed{322}$$

Order of Operations Example — (With Parentheses)

- If there are parentheses, the computer starts at the inner pair of parentheses and converts everything to a single number. Then the computer repeats the process with the next pair of parentheses working "inside" out.

Example:
((6 + 4) * 2) /4 =
([10]   * 2) /4 =
      [20] /4 = [5]

In-Class Exercise 4-1

You Try Some Now (Without Parentheses)

1) $2 \wedge 3 + 4 * 5 - 4/2 * 5 =$ _____
2) $14 - 2 * 2 + 6 - 2 * 3 * 2 =$ _____
3) $14/2 * 3 - 2 \wedge 3 + 4 =$ _____

Now try some with parentheses

1) $6 + (9 * 2) =$ _____
2) $(6 + (9 * 2)) * 5 =$ _____
3) $3 * ((4 + (6 * 2)) * (9/3 - 1)) =$ _____

A computer is not required here, but it could be used to check the answers. You don't need a line number for calculator mode. Simply type PRINT and the calculations you want done. Example: If you wish to multiply 2 asterisk 3, simply PRINT 2 * 3 and press RETURN. The answer (6) will be displayed.

Tips on Using Parentheses — Summary

- **When in doubt, use parentheses. They can't do any harm!**
  — Use parentheses around operations you want performed first
- **Make sure that every left parenthesis has a matching right parenthesis**
  — Count them to be sure!
- **Order of Operations**
  — Inner most pair of parentheses first (M.D.A.S. rule inside parentheses)
  — Then work "inside" out
  — In case of a "tie," computer starts to the left and works right doing exponentiation (∧) and the M.D.A.S. rule.

Variable Names Used with Applesoft BASIC

- Must begin with a letter (A-Z)
  — May be followed by another letter
          or
  —May be followed by a digit (0-9)
- Some examples of variable names include:
  — A, B, C, D, E, F, G, H, I, J, K, L, M, N, O, P, Q, R, S, T, U, V, W, X, Y, Z.
  — A1, A2, B1, B2, C3, C5, D9, N9, P4, Q1, R6, Y7
  — AA, AZ, GP, MU, ZZ, BB, XY, LL, FG, LE, RE
    (You get the picture! Using the above combinations, you can use approximately 900 variable names.)
- There are some words with special meaning in the BASIC language and they *cannot* be used as variable names.
  — The complete list of reserved words, which cannot be used in variable names, appears in Appendix B of the Applesoft Tutorial Manual and Appendix G of the Applesoft BASIC Programming Reference Manual.

In-Class Exercise 4-2
(Assigning Numeric Values to Variables)

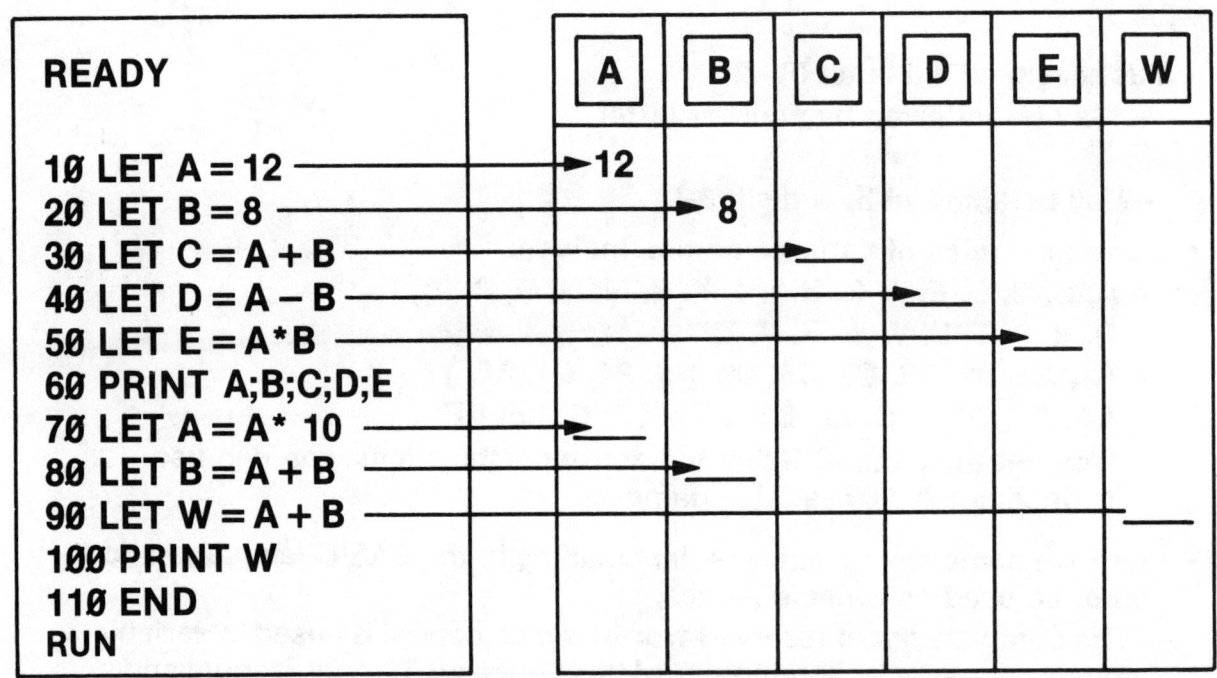

Basic Program for a Mathematical Operation

Line No.	Key Word[1]	Other Part of Statement	
10	LET	X = 5	**RETURN**
20	LET	Y = 12	**RETURN**
30	LET	Z = X*Y	**RETURN**
40	PRINT	Z	**RETURN**
99	END		

RUN

(1) LET is an optional key word for Applesoft BASIC. Some computers require you to use LET however. Beware of this if you use another computer.

Analysis of the BASIC Program for a Mathematical Operation

Line No.	Statement	Meaning to Computer
10	LET X = 5	Assign a value of 5 to variable X
20	LET Y = 12	Assign a value of 12 to variable Y
30	LET Z = X*Y	Take the values of X and Y, multiply them together, and assign the resulting value to the variable Z
40	PRINT Z	Print the value of Z (which is 60 in the example)
99	END	END PROGRAM
RUN		EXECUTE PROGRAM

A BASIC Mathematical Program
Area of Rectangle

YOUR ACTION

DISPLAY

1. Type NEW and press RETURN.
2. Type and enter.
   Line 5 clears the screen.

```
5 HOME
10 REM * AREA OF A RECTANGLE PROBLEM *
20 REM * AREA (A) = LENGTH (L) X WIDTH (W) *
30 LET L = 10
40 LET W = 5
50 LET A = L*W
60 PRINT A
```

3. Type RUN and press RETURN.

```
RUN
50
```

**NOTE THAT WE SAID IN LINE 60 PRINT A. There were no quotes around the letter A because we wanted the computer to PRINT the *value* of A.
If we wanted the computer to PRINT the exact word or letter, we would put quotes around the word or variable.**

Area of Rectangle Program Modified

YOUR ACTION	DISPLAY	
1. Add Line 7Ø to read then press RETURN	70 PRINT "AREA (IN SQ. IN.) IS", A	
2. Type RUN and press RETURN.	AREA (IN SQ. IN.) IS 5Ø	Ⓐ
3. Add Line 8Ø to read then press RETURN.	80 PRINT "THE AREA IS", A, "SQ. IN."	
4. Type RUN and press RETURN.	THE AREA IS 5Ø SQ. IN.	Ⓑ
5. Add Line 9Ø to read then press RETURN.	9Ø PRINT "THE AREA IS"; A; "SQ. IN."	
6. Type RUN and press RETURN.	100 PRINT "THE AREA IS ";A;" SQ. IN." THE AREA IS5ØSQ. IN. THE AREA IS 5Ø SQ. IN.	Ⓒ & Ⓓ

Notes:

Ⓐ Comma in Line 7Ø told the computer to print two separate items on the same line.

Ⓑ Commas in Line 8Ø told the computer to print three separate items on the same line.

Ⓒ In Line 9Ø, a semicolon tells the computer to print the output close together without spacing. But in line 100, we inserted a space between the word "is" and the second quotes ("). Also, we inserted a space between the third quote and the word "sq." Note the difference in the outputs.

Ⓓ LIST your program when you finish. Run your program several times and note that you have printed your answer five different ways.

Assignment 4-1

1. **Write a Program to Find Area of a Triangle**
   A. GIVEN: A = ½ bh WHERE b = 5, h = 10
   B. Include Remarks Statement
   C. Have Program PRINT "THE AREA = " (Your Answer) "SQ. FT."

2. **Write a Program to Find the Volume of a Rectangular Solid**
   A. GIVEN V = L*W*H, L = 5, W = 10, H = 2
   B. Include Remarks Statement
   C. Have Program PRINT "THE VOLUME = " (Your Answer) "CUBIC IN."

3. Given the formula for converting Fahrenheit to Celsius as follows:
$$C° = (F° - 32) \times (5/9)$$
   A. Write and RUN a program that converts 75° Fahrenheit to Celsius.
   B. Change the value of F from 75° to 45° and RUN the program again.

4. Given the formula for converting Celsius to Fahrenheit as follows:
$$F° = 9/5 \times C° + 32$$
   A. Write and RUN a program to find F if C is 20°.
   B. Change the value of C from 20° to 35° and RUN the program to find F.

Summary — Mathematical Operations

- **LET is an optional key word when using Applesoft BASIC.**
  — **Other computers using BASIC might require use of LET, so beware!**

- **10 PRINT A: Tells computer to print the value of A**
  — **Whereas 10 PRINT "A": Tells computer to print letter A (because the computer will print anything within quotes).**

- **A comma in a PRINT statement tells the computer to leave several spaces between items separated by the commas.**

- **A semicolon in a PRINT statement tells the computer to print the output close together without spacing.**

Print Zones

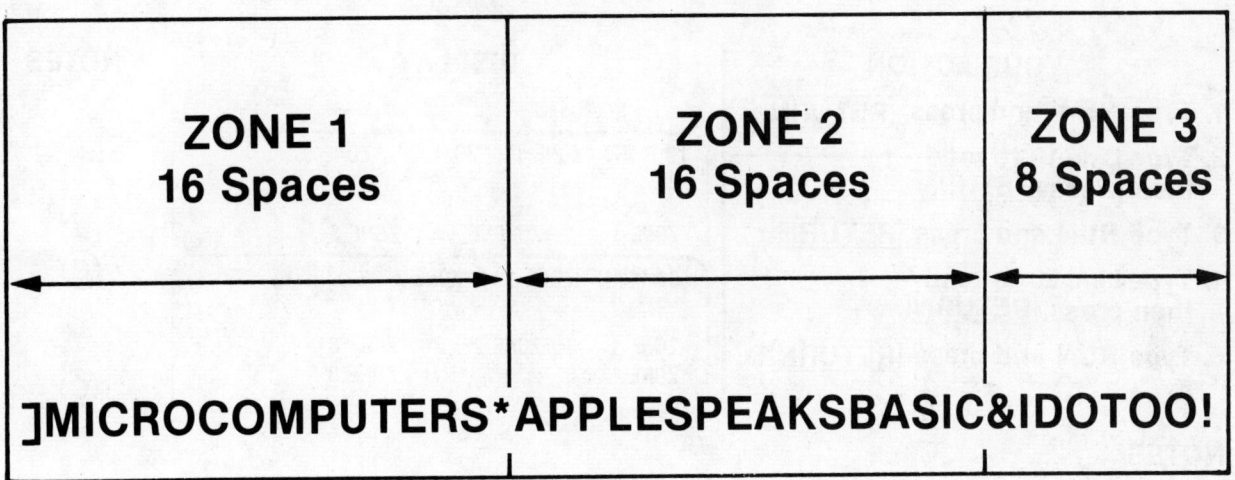

- **The Apple II is divided into three PRINT zones.**
  - **Each of the first two PRINT zones has 16 spaces for up to 16 characters.**
  - **The third PRINT zone has 8 spaces for up to 8 characters.**
  - **The Apple II can display up to 40 characters per line (2 × 16 + 8 = 40).**

Print Zones and the Use of Commas

YOUR ACTION	DISPLAY	NOTES
1. Type NEW and press RETURN.		
2. Type Line 10 to read then press RETURN.	10 PRINT "ZONE 1", "ZONE 2", "ZONE 3",	
3. Type RUN and press RETURN.	ZONE 1 ZONE 2 ZONE 3	Ⓐ Ⓑ
4. Type Line 20 to read then press RETURN.	20 PRINT "ZONE 1",, "ZONE 3"	
5. Type RUN and press RETURN.	ZONE 1 ZONE 2 ZONE 3 ZONE 1 ZONE 3	Ⓒ

NOTES

Ⓐ There are two (2) 16-character PRINT zones and one 8-character PRINT zone per line (since $2 \times 16 + 8 = 40$, the screen can display up to 40 characters per line).

Ⓑ Note that there are two commas between ZONE 1 and ZONE 3.

Ⓒ The comma tells the computer to move to the next PRINT zone each time a comma is encountered.

Semicolon vs. Comma

YOUR ACTION	THE DISPLAY READS:
1. Type NEW and press RETURN.	
2. Type exactly as shown then RETURN. →	10 PRINT "A"; "SEMICOLON"; "PACKS"; "ITEMS"; "CLOSE"; "TOGETHER"
3. Type exactly as shown then RETURN. →	20 PRINT "BUT A COMMA", "LEAVES", "SPACES"
4. Type RUN and press RETURN.	ASEMICOLONPACKSITEMSCLOSETOGETHER BUT A COMMA LEAVES SPACES
5. Type Lines 30, 40, 50, and 60 as shown then press RETURN. →	30 LET A = 5 40 LET B = 10 50 LET C = 15 60 PRINT A; B; C
6. Type RUN 30 and press RETURN.	51015

79

Use of the Semicolon — Summary

- The effect of the semicolon from computer to computer varies, but it is always true that a semicolon leaves less space between the answers or results printed than the COMMA.
- GENERAL RULE: when you want more than one item on the same line and
    - If you want your results or output spread out, use a comma.
    - If you want your results or output close together, use a semicolon.

PRACTICE 6

Area of a Rectangle Program

Part I

1. Enter and RUN this progam:
   ```
   10 REM**AREA OF A RECTANGLE PROGRAM**
   20 REM**AREA (A)=LENGTH(L)*WIDTH(W)**
   30 LET L=10
   40 LET W=5
   50 LET A=L*W
   60 PRINT A
   ```
2. Add a new program line to include a label on your answer. For example, the area of the rectangle is 50 square inches.
3. Add new program lines to PRINT the following:
   a. The length of the rectangle is 10 inches.
   b. The width of the rectangle is 5 inches.

Part II

1. *Do not* type NEW.
2. Change the values of L and W in the program. (Think before you change the lines! How many lines do you have to change? Change only those lines!)

PRACTICE 7

Program Using Mathematical Operators

1. Enter and RUN the following program:
   ```
   10 REM**MATH PROBLEMS**
   20 LET A=75
   30 LET B=50
   40 LET C=A+B
   50 PRINT C
   ```
2. Change the values of A and B in the program and RUN it. Fill in the results: A=_____, B=_____, C=_____.
3. Add a program line to label the answer. Example: "The sum is (your answer)."
4. Write a program to multiply (*) two numbers (any two).
5. Add the program line to PRINT: "The product of (your no.) "*" (your no.) "is" (your answer). Example: The product of 5 * 5 is 25.
6. Write a program to divide (/) two numbers (any two).
7. Add the program line to PRINT: "The quotient of" (your #) "/" (your #) is (your answer). Example: The quotient of 10/2 is 5.
8. Write a program to subtract (−) two numbers (any two).
9. Add the program line to PRINT: "The difference between "(your #) "−" (your #) is (your answer). Example: The difference between 10−5 is 5.

Additional practices for this Part will be found in the back of the book.

PART 5

Scientific Notation

What You Will Learn

To understand and use scientific notation.

Review and Feedback

The purpose of this part of the program is to evaluate students' overall performance and determine which students are having problems. The students who are having problems will be given the opportunity to review concepts they have not mastered. The review and feedback phase is divided into the following parts:

1. Exam — written/lab

2. Open discussion with students about their concerns and interests

3. Evaluation of student's performance

4. Recommendations

Scientific Notation

- Scientists often express large numbers like 186,000 and small numbers like 0.00015 as the product of two numbers. For example:

  a) $186{,}000 = 1.86 \times 10^5$
  b) $0.00015 = 1.5 \times 10^{-4}$
  c) $764{,}000 = 7.64 \times 10^5$
  d) $0.0347 = 3.47 \times 10^{-2}$
  e) $5{,}000{,}000 = 5 \times 10^6$

Scientific Notation

Ordinary Notation		Scientific Notation		Scientific Notation in Applesoft	Meaning
5,000,000,000	=	5×10^9	=	5E + 09	ADD 9 zeroes after 5
.000005	=	5×10^{-6}	=	5E − 06	Shift decimal 6 places to left
.00000005	=	5×10^{-8}	=	5E − 08	Shift decimal 8 places left
5 (with 15 zeroes)	=	5×10^{15}	=	5E + 15	ADD 15 zeroes after 5
5 (with 16 zeroes)	=	5×10^{16}	=	5E + 16	ADD 16 zeroes after 5

- Applesoft uses scientific notation for very large and very small numbers.
- Rule 1: E + 09 means move the decimal point 9 places to the right.
- Rule 2: E − 09 means move the decimal point 9 places to the left.

Assignment 5-1 — (Scientific Notation)

1. Type, enter, and RUN the following program:

    ```
     5 HOME
    10 PRINT 5000 000, 0.000005, .00000005, 5 000 000 000
    15 PRINT
    20 PRINT 5 000 000 000 000 000,  5 000 000 000 000 0000
                  (15 zeroes)                (16 zeroes)
    ```

2. Experiment with scientific notation until you feel comfortable with it.

Review and Feedback

A. Quiz — Written/Lab

B. Open discussion with students on concerns and interest

C. Evaluation of student's performance

D. Recommendations

FEEDBACK QUESTIONNAIRE

1. Do you like working with computers? _____ (yes, no) If not, why not? _____
   _____

2. What things do you like most about computers? _____
   _____

3. What do you dislike most about computers? _____
   _____

4. If you were a design engineer and could design the computer to do anything you wanted it to, what kinds of things would you include in your design? (Use your imagination!)
   _____
   _____

5. What was the hardest thing for you to understand about the computer so far? _____

6. What was the easiest thing for you to understand? _____
   _____

7. Were you afraid or nervous when you first used the computer? _____ (yes, no)

8. Do you feel comfortable using the computer now? _____ (yes, no)

9. Would you prefer to be doing something else rather than learning about computers? _____ (yes, no) If yes, what would you like to do? _____
   _____

10. Is the teacher going too fast, too slow, or just right for you? _____

11. Do you find the lessons interesting, boring, or so-so? _____

12. If you could teach this course, what would you do to make the lessons more interesting? _____
    _____

13. Have you decided what you want to do for a vocation? _____ (yes, no)
    If yes, what? _____

14. Would you like to take additional courses to learn more about computers and programming? _____ (yes, no)

15. Do you have any additional comments? _____
    _____
    _____
    _____
    _____
    _____

PRACTICE 8

Scientific Notation

1. Convert the following to standard scientific notation (example: $5,000,000 = 5 \times 10^6$):
   a. 5,165,123
   b. .000007
   c. .00000008
   d. 6,001,255
   e. 80 000 000 000 000 000 (16 zeros)
   f. 8000 000 000 000 000 (15 zeros)
   g. 9,000,156,000
   h. 7,701,777
   i. 77,701,777,000
   j. 5,612,345,000
2. Change the above numbers to computer scientific notation used in the Apple II (example: $5,000,000,000 = 5E+09$).

Note: The Apple will print a number in scientific notation if:
    A. For positive numbers
       1. The value is greater than 999999999
       2. The value is less than .01
    B. For negative numbers
       1. The value is less than -999999999
       2. The value is greater than $-.01$

Another way of indicating this is to say that the number will be printed in scientific notation if its *absolute value* is larger than 999999999 or less than .01.

PART 6

Relational Operators and IF-THEN/GOTO Statements

What You Will Learn

1. How computers compare (or relate) one value with another.

2. To explain the purpose and use of the six relational operators: =, >, <, <=, >=, <>.

3. To explain the purpose and use of the key words IF-THEN, GOTO.

4. To write, enter, and run programs that use IF-THEN and GOTO statements.

5. To understand and use the counting program.

Relational Operators

- **Allow computer to compare one value with another.**
  - The three relational operators include

Symbol	Meaning	Examples
=	Equal	A = B
>	Greater than	A > B
<	Less than	A < B

  - Combining the three operators above we have

Symbol	Meaning	Examples
<>	Is not equal to	A <> B
<=	Less than or equal to	A <= B
>=	Greater than or equal to	A >= B

NOTE: To distinguish between < and >, just remember that the smaller part of the < symbol points to the smaller of two quantities being compared.

IF-THEN

- IF-THEN is used in conditional branching.
  - That is, the program will "branch" to another part of the program on the condition that it passes the test it contains.
  - If the test fails, the program simply continues to the next line.
- Example:

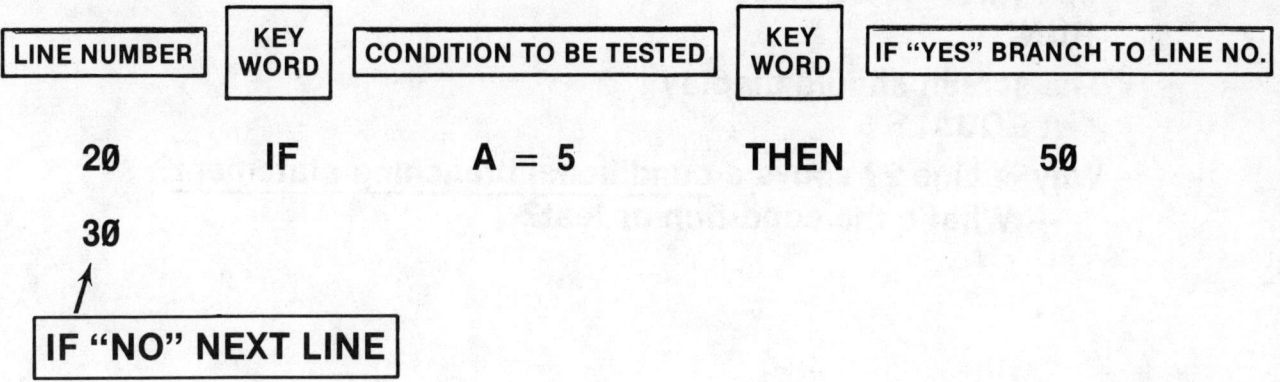

Sample Program Using IF-THEN (Conditional Branching)

- Program
  ```
  10 LET A = 5
  20 IF A = 5 THEN 50
  30 PRINT "A DOES NOT EQUAL 5."
  40 END
  50 PRINT "A EQUALS 5."
  RUN
  ```
- The screen should display
  A EQUALS 5
- Why is Line 20 above a <u>conditional branching statement?</u>
  — What's the condition or test?

In-Class Exercise 6-1 (IF-THEN)

Given: A = 10, B = 20, C = 30
Exercises:

Exercise No.	Statement	Condition is (T or F)	Branch to (Line N) Ⓐ
1.	10 IF A = B THEN 40	F	20
2.	10 IF A <> B THEN 50	T	50
3.	10 IF A > B THEN 60	F	20
4.	10 IF A < B THEN 70	T	70
5.	10 IF C < = A + B THEN 80	T	80
6.	10 IF C > = A + B THEN 90	T	90
7.	10 IF B > A THEN 100	T	100
8.	10 IF B/A > = C/A THEN 110	F	20
9.	10 IF A * B < = A * C THEN 120	T	120
10.	10 IF C/A < = A * B THEN 130	T	130

Ⓐ Note: If condition is false (F), the computer will execute the next line (i.e., 20).

A Counting Program — Using IF-THEN

- Program
   ```
   10 LET J = 0
   20 LET J = J + 1
   30 PRINT J
   40 IF J < 10 THEN 20
   RUN
   OUTPUT IS*
   ```
- In-Class Exercise 6-2
   Modify above program to count to 50 by 5's

```
* OUTPUT
   1
   2
   3
   4
   5
   6
   7
   8
   9
  10
```

IF-THEN Counter Program Analysis

	PROGRAM EXECUTION	"J" COUNTER STATUS	DISPLAY
INITIALIZE	10 J = 0	0	
1ST TIME	20 J = J + 1	1 = 0 + 1	
	30 PRINT J,		
	40 IF J < 4 THEN 20		
2ND TIME	20 J = J + 1	2 = 1 + 1	
	30 PRINT J,		
	40 IF J < 4 THEN 20		
3RD TIME	20 J = J + 1	3 = 2 + 1	
	30 PRINT J,		
4TH TIME	40 IF J < 4 THEN 20	4 = 3 + 1	
	20 J = J + 1		
	30 PRINT J		
	40 IF J < 4 THEN 20		
END	50 END		1 2 3 4

IF-THEN COUNTER — Program Analysis (Stop-Action)

	PROGRAM EXECUTION	"J" COUNTER STATUS	DISPLAY
INITIALIZE	10 J = 0	10 [0]	
1ST TIME	20 J = J + 1	20 [1] = 0 + 1	
	30 PRINT J	30	[1]
	40 STOP		
	45 REM** TYPE CONT TO CONTINUE**		
	50 IF J < 4 THEN 20		
2ND TIME	20 J = J + 1	20 [2] = 1 + 1	
	30 PRINT J	30	[2]
	40 STOP		
	45 REM		
	50 IF J < 4 THEN 20		
3RD TIME	20 J = J + 1	20 [3] = 2 + 1	
	30 PRINT J	30	[3]
	40 STOP		
	45 REM		
	50 IF J < 4 THEN 20		
4TH TIME	20 J = J + 1	20 [4] = 3 + 1	
	30 PRINT J	30	[4]
	40 STOP		
	45 REM		
	50 IF J < 4 THEN 20		
END	60 END		

In-Class Exercise 6-3
(GOTO — Unconditional Branching)

- Type and RUN this program:
  ```
  10 HOME
  20 PRINT "YOUR NAME";
  30 GOTO 20
  ```
- What happened?
  — Do you know how to stop the program? (What about the CTRL and C keys!)
  Explain this simple program (Line 10 merely clears the screen). But what does Line 30 tell the computer to do?
  -- Were there any tests or conditions to be satisfied in Line 30 before it does what it has to do?
  — Do you understand now why the GOTO statement is called an unconditional branching statement?
- Don't leave this page until you understand everything!

Exercise 6-4 (GOTO/IF-THEN)

Exercise:
- Study the program below and write the message that would be printed if the program were executed.

```
10 PRINT "WELCOME TO LEEDS MIDDLE SCHOOL"
20 GOTO 70
25 PRINT
30 PRINT "HELLO SUPERSTAR"
35 PRINT
40 PRINT "COMPUTERS ARE MY THING"
50 GOTO 100
60 IF A = 5 THEN 90
70 PRINT "COMPUTER WORKSHOP"
80 GOTO 40
90 GOTO 120
100 LET A = 5
110 GOTO 60
120 PRINT "AND I'M A SUPERSTAR!"
130 END
140 PRINT "APPLE II MICROCOMPUTER"
150 PRINT "I CAN DO IT TOO"
160 PRINT "I SPEAK BASIC"
```

Assignment 6-1

1. **Read pages 55 (The Truth) and 59 (The IF Statement) in the** *Applesoft Tutorial.*

2. **Write a program of your choice using conditional (IF-THEN) and unconditional (GOTO) statements.**

3. **Write a counting program.**
   — Count to 100 by 10's.

What We Have Learned — Summary

- **Relational operators:** $=, >, <, <>, <=, >=$
- **IF-THEN**
- **GOTO (No space between GO and TO)**
- **Conditional Branching**
  - If condition is met, (i.e., TRUE), branch to designated line in program.
  - If condition is not met, (i.e., FALSE), go to next line number in program.
- **Unconditional branching**
  - GOTO line XX (no conditions or tests required)
  - A GOTO statement, as the name implies, forces the computer to go to a specific statement anywhere in the program.

PRACTICE 9

Using IF-THEN

Part I.

1. Enter and RUN the following program:
    ```
    10  LET A=10
    20  IF A=10 THEN 50
    30  PRINT "A DOES NOT EQUAL 10"
    40  END
    50  PRINT "A EQUALS 10"
    ```
2. Change Line 10 to Let A=5 and then RUN it.
3. Change Line 10 to Let A=3 and then RUN it.

Part II.

1. Using this program as an example, write a new program to PRINT A EQUALS 3 and RUN it.
2. Change the values of A in Line 10 and RUN the program several times.

PRACTICE 10

Counting Program Using IF-THEN

1. Enter and RUN this program:
    ```
    10  LET  J=0
    20  LET  J=J+1
    30  PRINT J
    40  IF J<10 THEN 20
    ```
2. Write a program to count from 1 to 15.
3. Write a program to count to 50 by 5's.
4. Write a program to count to 100 by 10's
5. Write a program to count from 15 to 30 and PRINT the answers in one column (vertically).
    Example: 15
              16
              17
              18
              and so forth
6. Write a program to count from 20 to 40. PRINT answers horizontally in three columns.
    Example:
              20   21   22
              23   24   25
              and so forth

PART 7

Input Statements

What You Will Learn

1. To explain the purpose and use of key words input, input with built-in print.

2. To explain the purpose and use of a trailing semicolon on a program line.

3. To identify and use string variables A$, B$, C$, and so forth.

4. To explain the difference between numeric and string variables.

5. To write, enter, and run programs that use the concepts of this lesson.

Input Statement

STATEMENT

10 INPUT A

FUNCTION

- Causes the computer to stop, PRINT a ?, and wait for you to type in a decimal number.
- After you type in a value for A, the computer continues the program when you press the RETURN key.

Input Statements

YOUR ACTION

1. Type NEW and press RETURN.
2. Type and enter Lines 5 & 10 as shown.
3. Type RUN and press RETURN.
4. Enter a number (e.g., type 5 and enter).
5. RUN this program several times to get the feel of it.

DISPLAY

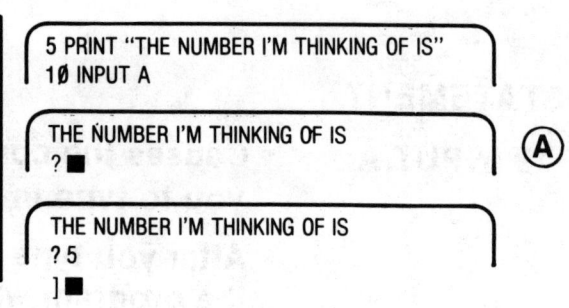

```
5 PRINT "THE NUMBER I'M THINKING OF IS"
10 INPUT A
```

```
THE NUMBER I'M THINKING OF IS
?■
```
(A)

```
THE NUMBER I'M THINKING OF IS
? 5
]■
```

(A) The question mark on the screen means, "It's your turn and I'm waiting."

Input Statements with Built-In Print

YOUR ACTION | DISPLAY

1. Add a semicolon to Line 5 of the resident program (i.e., the program now residing in the computer).
2. RUN the program again.
3. Change Line 5 to read:
4. Delete Line 10 by typing 10 and then press RETURN .
5. RUN the program.

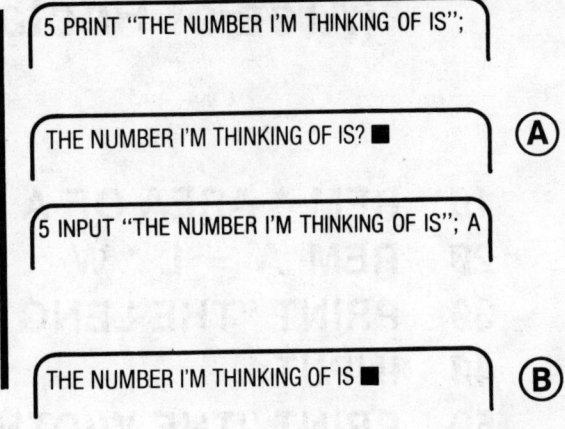

```
5 PRINT "THE NUMBER I'M THINKING OF IS";

THE NUMBER I'M THINKING OF IS? ■         Ⓐ

5 INPUT "THE NUMBER I'M THINKING OF IS"; A

THE NUMBER I'M THINKING OF IS ■          Ⓑ
```

Ⓐ Note that the semicolon puts the question mark on the same line.

Ⓑ The results are exactly the same as before. But here is what was changed:
— PRINT TO INPUT (Line 5)
— Eliminated Line 10
— Eliminated ? after "is." (If you want a question mark, you can add it. Do you know how?)

Input Statements — (Area of Rectangle Program)

```
10    REM * AREA OF A RECTANGLE PROBLEM*
20    REM  A = L * W
30    PRINT "THE LENGTH IS"
40    INPUT L
50    PRINT "THE WIDTH IS"
60    INPUT W
70    A = L * W
80    PRINT "THE AREA IS"
90    PRINT A
```

Area of Rectangle Problem Revisited
(Using Input Statements)

YOUR ACTION

DISPLAY

1. Type in program Lines 10 through 60 as shown.

```
10 REM * AREA OF A RECTANGLE PROBLEM *
20 INPUT "THE LENGTH IS "; L
30 INPUT "THE WIDTH IS "; W
40 A = L * W
50 PRINT "THE AREA IS ";
60 PRINT A
```
(A)

2. Type RUN then press RETURN.
3. Type in the length (say 10) and enter.
4. Type in the width and press RETURN.
5. What is your answer?

```
THE LENGTH IS ■
THE LENGTH IS 10
THE WIDTH IS ■
```
(B)

(A) Note the trailing semicolon. It is used to hook Lines 50 and 60 together.

(B) Note that the program waits for an input from the keyboard. If you don't enter a number or press RETURN, it will just stay at that line until the machine is turned off or reset.

Assignment 7-1

Write a simple program to do the following:
(using input statement)
a) Input your age
b) Input your zip code
c) Input your weight
d) Input your height in inches
e) PRINT each of the above with the proper labels
   (for example: My age is 15 or I am 15 years old).

What We Have Learned

- Trailing semicolon hooks two lines together.
- Input statements cause the computer to stop and wait for an input from the keyboard.
- Input statements can have a built-in message to tell you what to input.

Numeric vs. String Variables

Numeric Variable		Declaration Character'⁽¹⁾		String Variable
A	+	$	=	A$
A1	+	$	=	A1$
AB	+	$	=	AB$
AZ	+	$	=	AZ$

(1) **NOTE: Simply by adding the string declaration character ($) to the numeric variable allows you to use any numeric variable as a string variable.**

Example of Use of String Variables

YOUR ACTION | DISPLAY

1. Type and enter.

```
10 HOME
20 INPUT "YOUR NAME IS "; A$
30 PRINT "HELLO THERE, "; A$
```

2. Type **RUN** and press `RETURN`.

```
YOUR NAME IS ■
HELLO THERE, BILL
```
Ⓐ

Ⓐ **NOTE:**
It will print your name and not "BILL," unless your name is "BILL."

In-Class Exercise 7-1 (String Variables)

YOUR ACTION	DISPLAY
1. Type and enter.	5 HOME 10 INPUT "YOUR FIRST NAME" ; A$ 20 INPUT "YOUR MIDDLE NAME" ; B$ 30 INPUT "YOUR LAST NAME"; C$ 40 PRINT A$;" "; B$;" "; C$ 50 INPUT "YOUR FULL NAME"; D$ 60 PRINT D$ Ⓐ
2. Type RUN and press RETURN. (Sample)	YOUR FIRST NAME? AUBREY YOUR MIDDLE NAME? BRIGHT YOUR LAST NAME? JONES AUBREY BRIGHT JONES YOUR FULL NAME? AUBREY BRIGHT JONES AUBREY BRIGHT JONES

Ⓐ NOTES
You can add string variables together.
You must insert a space between string variables using " " marks.
A semicolon will not cause a space to be printed.

Assignment 7-2 (String Variables)

1. RUN and analyze the following program:

   ```
   10  INPUT "YOUR NAME IS" ; A$
   20  INPUT "YOUR HOUSE NUMBER" ; A
   30  INPUT "YOUR STREET NAME" ; B$
   40  INPUT "YOUR ZIP CODE" ; B
   50  PRINT A$
   60  PRINT A; " " ; B$
   70  PRINT "ZIP CODE" ; B
   ```

2. Answer the following questions:
   a) Why were A$ and B$ (string variables) required in Lines 10 and 30?
   b) Why were quotes (" ") inserted in Line 60?
   c) Why didn't we use $ symbol (or string declaration character) with A and B in Lines 20 and 40?

String Variables — Summary

- String variables can be assigned to indicate letters, words, and/or combinations of letters.
- It is possible to string up to 255 characters per string variable.
- String variables can be added together.
- Use " " marks to insert a space between string variables.

PRACTICE 11

Area of Rectangle Problem (Using INPUT Statement)

1. Enter and RUN this program:
   ```
   10  REM*AREA OF RECTANGLE PROBLEM*
   20  INPUT "THE LENGTH IS"; L
   30  INPUT "THE WIDTH IS"; W
   40  LET A = L*W
   50  PRINT "THE AREA IS"; A
   ```
2. Write a new program using INPUT statements to find volume (volume = length × width × height).
3. Include a statement: The volume is _____.

PRACTICE 12

More INPUT Statement Programs

Part I.

1. Write a program using INPUT statements to change meters to centimeters (centimeters = 100 × meters).
2. Include a statement: _____ meters equals _____ centimeters.

Part II.

1. Write a new program using INPUT statements to do the following:
   a. Input the number of members of your family.
   b. Input the age of the oldest member.
   c. Input the age of the youngest member.
   d. Input the average age of your family.
2. PRINT each with the proper labels.
   Example: The youngest member of my family is…

PRACTICE 13

String Variables

Part I.

1. Enter and RUN the following program:
   ```
   10  INPUT "THE CITY I LIVE IN IS ";A$
   20  INPUT "THE POPULATION OF MY CITY IS APPROXIMATELY ";A
   30  INPUT "THE STATE I LIVE IN IS ";B$
   40  INPUT "THE POPULATION OF MY STATE IS APPROXIMATELY ";B
   50  PRINT A$
   60  PRINT A;" ";B$
   70  PRINT "THE POPULATION OF THE STATE IS ";B
   ```
2. Answer the following questions:
   a. Why are A$ and B$ (string variables) required in Lines 10 and 30?
   b. Why were quotes (" ") inserted in Line 60?
   c. Why didn't we use $ symbol (or string declaration character) with A and B in Lines 20 and 40?

Part II.

1. Write a new program using INPUT statements, string variables, and a space between each line. PRINT all information (example: My best friend is _____) to give the following information:
   a. Your best friend.
   b. Your favorite subject.
   c. Your favorite food.
   d. Your favorite movie star.
   e. Your favorite color.
   f. Your zodiac sign.

PART 8

Using the Calculator Mode and Sizing Memory

What You Will Learn

1. To define and use the terms bit, byte, k, kbytes.

2. To determine how much memory is used in a BASIC program.

3. To explain the purpose and use of the command PRINT FRE (Ø).

4. To use the Apple II in calculator mode (i.e., without having to write a program).

BIT = **BINARY—DIGIT**

BIT = SMALLEST MEMORY CELL IN A COMPUTER

BIT = "1" OR "Ø"

1

MEMORY CELL WITH 1 BIT

8 MEMORY CELLS

0	1	1	0	1	0	1	1

8 BITS = 1 BYTE

BYTE = 8 BITS

K = 1000

KBYTES = 1000 BYTES

KBYTES = 8000 BITS

How Much Memory Is Used in BASIC Programs

WHAT'S STORED	HOW MUCH MEMORY	
1 ALPHA CHARACTER (A-Z)	1 BYTE	
1 SPECIAL CHARACTER (e.g., ", !, +, −, etc.)	1 BYTE	
1 NUMERIC CHARACTER (0-9)	1 BYTE	
1 SPACE	2 BYTES	
1 RETURN KEY AND OTHER	3 BYTES	MEMORY
1 RESERVE WORD SUCH AS FOR, GOTO, PRINT	1 BYTE	OVERHEAD*

EXAMPLE:

10	PRINT	"MY NAME IS AUBREY"	RETURN	
2* + 1*	+ 1 + 1*	19	1*	= 25 BYTES

*Included as part of memory overhead. Memory overhead means you will use 5 bytes of memory for each line, short or long.

NOTE! The above is just an exercise to help you understand memory allocation. You don't have to count bytes to determine how much memory was used. (Page 122 will show you an easy way to find out how much memory is available for your use.)

The Memory Command

- **PRINT FRE (0)**
  — This command is used to let you know how much memory is available to you.

  — Sometimes it may be important to know how much memory you are using for a given program.

  — If the amount of memory available in the Apple II you are using is 16k, this means that there are about 16,000 different memory locations to store and process your programs (actually 16,384).

- **Note!**
  — With no program loaded, there are less than 16,384 memory locations available for use. The difference in memory space, between actual space and 16,384, is set aside for processing programs and overall management and monitoring of what the computer is doing.

  — Also, your Apple II might have more than 16k of memory. So make certain you know how much memory you have in your computer. (The next page will show you how to determine the amount of memory available to you.)

Assignment 8-1

1. **Determining available memory:**
   a) Type NEW and press RETURN.
   b) Type PRINT FRE (0) and press RETURN.
   c) Display reads: * _____
   d) Now type the following and enter 10 PRINT "LEEDS MIDDLE SCHOOL."
   e) Type PRINT FRE (0) and press RETURN.
   f) How much space is left in memory? _____

2. (Optional) Read pages 53, 118, and 119 in the *Applesoft BASIC Programming Reference Manual.*

3. Use Apple II in calculator or immediate mode to solve the following:
   a) 25 * 4/2
   b) (25 + 6) − 7 + (2 * 5)
   c) 7/2 * 5 * 2 ∧ 3
   d) Any other problems you want to try

*If the number of free memory bytes exceeds 32, 767, FRE (0) returns a negative number. Adding 65,536 to FRE (0) will give you the actual number of free bytes of memory.
(Example: PRINT FRE (0) + 65536)

Remember! You don't need a line number for calculator mode. Simply type PRINT and the calculations you want done. Example: If you wish to multiply 2 asterisk 3, simply type PRINT 2 * 3, and press RETURN. The answer (6) will be displayed.

What We Have Learned

- COMPUTERS SPEAK IN MACHINE LANGUAGE

- MACHINE LANGUAGE IS A FORM OF BINARY CODING

- BINARY CODE CAN BE EITHER "0" OR "1" BITS

- BIT = BINARY DIGIT

- BYTE = 8 BITS

- YOU DO NOT HAVE TO KNOW MACHINE LANGUAGE TO USE COMPUTERS!

PRACTICE 14

Sizing Memory and Calculator Mode

Part I.

1. To determine available memory:
   a. Type NEW and press RETURN.
   b. Type PRINT FRE (0) and press RETURN.
   c. Display reads: _____.*
   d. Now type the following and enter   10 PRINT "LEEDS MIDDLE SCHOOL."
   e. Type PRINT FRE (0) and press RETURN.
   f. How much space is left in memory? _____

Part II.

1. Use Apple II in calculator or immediate mode to solve the following:
   a. 25 * 4/2
   b. (25 + 6) − 7 + (2 * 5)
   c. 7/2 * 5 * 2 ∧ 3
   d. Any other problems you want to try.

*If you get a negative number, type the following:
   PRINT FRE (0) + 65536

PART 9
Using the Disk Drive

What You Will Learn

1. How to use the disk drive as an output device to save information stored in memory.

2. How to use the disk drive as an input device to load information from disk to memory.

3. To explain and use the commands SAVE, LOAD, and RUN.

4. To practice using the disk drive.

The Disk Drive as an I/O Device

- The disk drive is an input/output (I/O) device which allows you to "save" programs on a disk or "load" programs from a disk.
- The disks you will use with the Apple are square pieces of plastic (5¼" on a side) which are specially treated so that they can store information from the Apple.
- When you pick up a disk, it is very important that you touch only the disk cover and NEVER TOUCH THE DISK SURFACE (or else the programs on the disk may be destroyed). IF YOU ARE NOT FAMILIAR WITH THE HANDLING OF A DISK, REFER TO PAGES 5-7 OF THE APPLE DOS MANUAL.
- After you store a program on a disk, you will probably want to write your name on the disk label. Be sure to use a soft-tip pen when writing on the disk label.
- Since the Apple can send and retrieve information to and from a disk at a much faster rate than to and from a tape, whenever possible it's much better to use a disk. However, there are special steps to follow to make sure that your disk is ready to be used. These steps are called INITIALIZING THE DISK.

Initializing a Disk

STEP   ACTION

1. Be sure the Apple is turned off.
2. Open the disk drive door by gently lifting the door from the bottom. (If you have more than one disk drive, you must use Drive #1.)
3. Insert the Apple Master Disk* which comes with the disk drive. (See the diagram on page 7 of the Apple DOS manual if you're not sure how to insert the disk.)
4. Close the drive door by gently pushing down on the door.
5. Turn on the Apple. (You will notice the red light on the disk drive come on and the disk will whirr for a few seconds.)
6. After the disk drive light goes off, you will see a message on the screen telling you that the Apple Master Disk is now ready to be used. (However, we don't want to use the Master Disk itself. Actually, all we wanted was to have the Apple DOS [Disk Operating System] placed in the Apple memory. The DOS tells the Apple that you will be using a disk to "save" and "load" programs. Without the DOS the Apple would not even be able to turn on the disk drive!)

*NOTE: Instead of the Apple Master Disk, you can use any disk that has already been INITIALIZED (since it will contain the Apple DOS).

Using the Disk Drive as an Input Device
(That is, loading a program from disk)

STEP	ACTION
1.	Turn the Apple off and then on again to boot your disk. You should see your greeting program displayed.
2.	Type LOAD NUMBER-2 and press RETURN . (But don't use quotes, and be sure to use the hyphen.) After the disk drive whirrs for a while, you will hear a beep and see a message that says FILE NOT FOUND. The Apple calls all saved programs FILES. Here, it is telling you that you spelled the name of your program differently from the way you spelled it when you saved it. (Remember you called it NUMBER 2; no hyphen.)
3.	Now type LOAD NUMBER 2 and press RETURN . The disk drive will come on and then stop. It will seem as though nothing has happened, although quite a bit has actually taken place. You will find that your greeting program has been erased from the Apple's memory and been replaced by the program which you called NUMBER 2. To verify that this is so, type RUN and you will see the message from program NUMBER 2 displayed on the screen.
4.	Now type NEW, press RETURN , and type RUN. Nothing will happen. This is because when you type NEW, the Apple's memory is erased and whatever program was stored there is lost.
5.	Now type RUN NUMBER 2 and press RETURN . The disk drive will come on, and the message from your program NUMBER 2 is displayed on the screen. When using the disk, it is possible to RUN a program directly without first typing LOAD.

Using the Disk Drive as an Output Device
(That is, saving a program on disk)

Actually, in a way you've already saved two programs on disk: your "greeting" program; and the Apple DOS [Disk Operating System] instructions (which were automatically saved). Now you will learn how to "save" other programs as well.

STEP	ACTION
1.	Boot* your disk.
2.	Type NEW.
3.	Enter the following program.

```
 5 HOME
10 REM THIS IS MY SECOND PROGRAM
20 PRINT "I HAVE LEARNED HOW TO INITIALIZE A DISK."
30 PRINT
40 PRINT "WHEN A DISK IS INITIALIZED, THE APPLE DOS"
50 PRINT
60 PRINT "IS AUTOMATICALLY LOADED INTO THE APPLE'S
    MEMORY."
```

4. Type SAVE NUMBER 2 AND PRESS [RETURN]. The disk drive will whirr and your program is now saved.
5. Type CATALOG and you will see your new program listed along with your greeting program.
6. Open the disk drive door and remove the Master Disk.
7. Place your blank disk in the drive and close the drive door.
8. You're now ready to initialize your own disk. The initialization process consists of two parts. The first is to print a "greeting" message which will appear on the screen when your disk is used. The second part is to have the DOS [Disk Operating System] instructions saved on your disk.
9. To create your "greeting" message, first type NEW.
10. Then write a small program such as the following:

```
10 REM THIS IS MY GREETING PROGRAM
20 HOME
30 VTAB 10
40 PRINT "THIS IS MY NAME'S DISK"
50 PRINT
60 PRINT "INITIALIZED TODAY'S DATE"
```

11. Now type, INIT YOUR NAME'S DISK and press [RETURN]. The disk drive will whirr for 30 seconds and then stop. Your disk is now initialized and the Apple DOS is automatically saved on your disk. To see if your disk has initialized properly, do the following.
12. Turn the Apple off.
13. Turn the Apple on again. (Be sure that your disk is still in the drive). You should hear the disk whirr for a few seconds and your greeting program should appear on the screen.
14. Now type CATALOG and press [RETURN]. The disk should whirr and a listing of all the programs contained on the disk should appear. In this case, the only program on the disk is your greeting program.

The "A" next to your greeting program on the CATALOG listing indicates that the program is written in the language called Applesoft. In this book this is the only computer language we will be using, although the Apple is capable of "understanding" many other computer languages as well.

*Boot refers to starting up the Apple and loading in the DOS [Disk Operating System] instructions from a disk.

PRACTICE 15

Using the Computer to Solve Problems

1. Write a program to solve the following problem. Include a PRINT statement in your program to describe your answer (output).
   The total enrollment at Armstrong High School is 1,264. There are 367 freshmen, 322 sophomores, and 298 juniors. How many seniors are there?
2. Write a new program using INPUT statements to solve one of the problems.

PRACTICE 16

Finding the Average Problems

1. Write a program to solve the following problem. Include a PRINT statement in your program to describe your answer.
   The weights of three boys are 140 lb, 150 lb, and 130 lb. What is their average weight?
2. Write a new program using INPUT statements to solve the same problem. (That is, you should use the INPUT statement for the weight of the three boys.)

PRACTICE 17

Using the Computer to Solve Problems

1. Write two programs to solve the following problems. Label your answers.
2. Over a period of six years Mr. Smith drove his car 53,862 miles. What was the average distance each year?
3. After 12 dozen bulbs were sold, how many of the 1,000 bulbs were left?

PART 10

Using FOR-NEXT-STEP Statements

What You Will Learn

1. To explain the purpose and use of key words FOR-NEXT, STEP.

2. To explain the purpose and use of the terms increment, decrement, initialize.

3. To compare key words GOTO, IF-THEN, FOR-NEXT and explain how they relate to one another.

4. To explain the purpose and use of timer loops.

For-Next Statement

- **Allows the computer to do the same thing over and over any number of times (and do it very fast!)**

FOR – NEXT Loop

YOUR ACTION	DISPLAY
1. Type and enter program as shown.	5 HOME 10 FOR J = 1 TO 10 20 PRINT " AUBREY " ; J 30 NEXT J
2. Type RUN and press RETURN.	AUBREY 1 AUBREY 2 AUBREY 3 AUBREY 4 AUBREY 5 AUBREY 6 AUBREY 7 AUBREY 8 AUBREY 9 AUBREY 10

FOR-NEXT-STEP Loop

YOUR ACTION   **DISPLAY**

1. Retype and enter Line 10 of resident* program as shown. ⟶

   ```
   10 FOR J = 1 TO 10 STEP 3
   ```
   Ⓐ

2. Type RUN and press RETURN.

   ```
   AUBREY 1
   AUBREY 4
   AUBREY 7
   AUBREY 10
   ```

*Resident means program currently in memory.

Ⓐ If step is not included in the statement, an increment of 1 is assigned by the computer (i.e., step 1).

Example of Program Statements Using Key Words

FOR-NEXT-STEP

```
10   FOR J = 10 TO 1 STEP -1
20   PRINT J;" ";
30   NEXT J
```

RUN
DISPLAY READS:
10 9 8 7 6 5 4 3 2 1

Analysis of FOR-NEXT-STEP Statements

LINE NO.	KEY WORD	COUNTER VARIABLE		INITIAL VALUE	FINAL VALUE	INCREMENT/ DECREMENT
10	FOR	J	=	10 TO	1	STEP -1
20	PRINT	J				
30	NEXT	J				

The FOR-NEXT-STEP loop works as follows: The first time the FOR statement is executed, the counter is set for the initial value "10." Then it executes Line 20 (PRINT J). When the program reaches Line 30 (NEXT J), the counter is decremented by the amount specified (Step-1). If this step has a positive value, the counter is incremented by the amount specified (e.g., Step 2 means increment by 2's).

Comparison of GOTO , IF-THEN , and FOR-NEXT Program Loops

A. GOTO
(Unconditional Loop)

```
 5 HOME
10 PRINT "AUBREY"
20 GOTO 10
RUN
```

- Program loops one zillion times!
  (or until you stop it)

B. IF-THEN
(Conditional Loop)

```
 5 HOME
10 LET J = 0
20 J = J + 1
30 IF J>6 THEN 99
40 PRINT "AUBREY  "; J
50 GOTO 20
99 END
RUN
```

- This program loops 6 times!

C. FOR-NEXT
(Conditional Loop)

```
 5 HOME
10 FOR J = 1 TO 6
20 PRINT = "AUBREY  "; J
30 NEXT J
99 END
RUN
```

- This program loops 6 times!

Comparison of GOTO , IF-THEN , and FOR-NEXT Program Loops

A. "DUMB LOOP"

AUBREY
AUBREY
AUBREY
AUBREY
AUBREY
AUBREY
AUBREY
AUBREY
AUBREY
AUBREY
AUBREY
AUBREY
AUBREY
AUBREY
AUBREY
AUBREY

B. "SMART LOOP"

AUBREY 1
AUBREY 2
AUBREY 3
AUBREY 4
AUBREY 5
AUBREY 6

C. "SMART LOOP"

AUBREY 1
AUBREY 2
AUBREY 3
AUBREY 4
AUBREY 5
AUBREY 6

NOTE: Press CTRL and C Keys to Get Out of Loop.

FOR-NEXT SUMMARY

- FOR – NEXT – STEP

— FOR – NEXT is always used as a pair.
— If the key word "step" is not used, the increment of 1 is assumed.
— If the step has a negative value, the counter is decremented (e.g., for J = 10 to 1 step -1).
— If the step has a positive value, the counter is incremented (e.g., for J = 4 to 10 step 2).

Flowchart Symbols

 • **Begin or End**

 • **Processing Block**

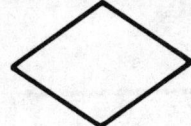 • **Decision Diamond**

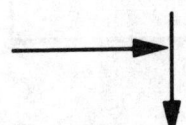 • **Connector Arrows**

GOTO-LOOP
(Unconditional)

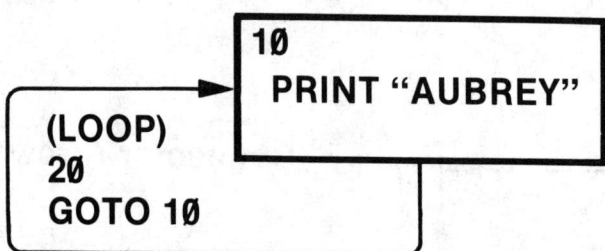

Looping with IF-THEN

FUNCTION

- **Clears Screen** — `5 HOME`
- **Initialized Program** — `10 LET J = 0`
- **Counter** — `20 J = J + 1`
- **Decision Block** — IS J > 6 ?
  - NO → `30 PRINT "AUBREY"; J` (LOOP) → `50 GOTO 20`
  - YES → `99 END`

Looping with FOR-NEXT

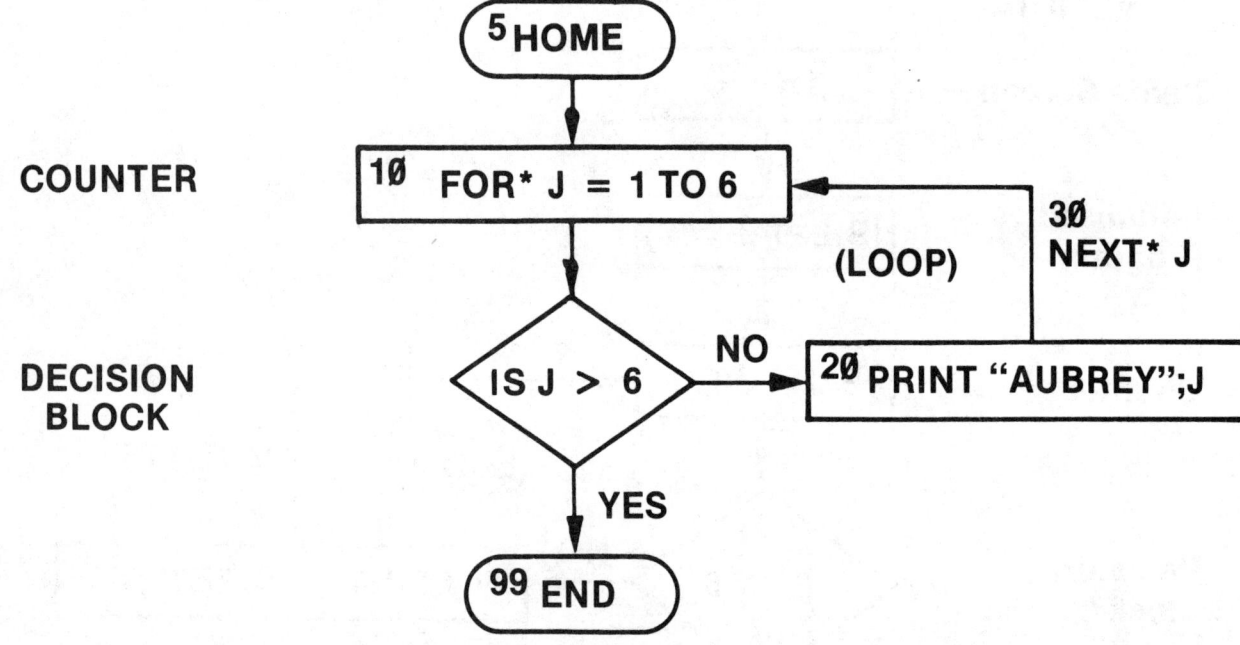

*FOR-NEXT *Work together as a counter

Timer Loop

- The Apple II can do approximately 750 FOR-NEXT loops per second.
- Example
    ```
    5 REM* 10 SECOND TIMER PROGRAM*
    10 PRINT "TIMER PROGRAM COUNTING"
    20 FOR X = 1 TO 7500
    30 NEXT X
    40 PRINT "TIMER PROGRAM ENDED"
    ```
- You don't believe the Apple II can count? Well, try it! (Type in the above program and RUN.)
    - Don't forget to use your watch!

Assignment 10-1

1. Type, enter, and RUN the following program.

   ```
   5    HOME
   10   PRINT "INPUT A VALUE N" : PRINT:PRINT
   15   INPUT "ENTER 1500, 2500, 3500 or 7500"; N
   20   HOME
   25   PRINT "THIS IS A DEMONSTRATION OF"
   30   PRINT:PRINT
   35   FOR J=1 TO N: NEXT
   40   PRINT "USING A FOR-NEXT TIMER LOOP"
   45   PRINT:PRINT:PRINT:PRINT
   50   FOR J=1 TO N: NEXT
   60   PRINT "IF YOU WISH TO CHANGE THE DISPLAY'S SPEED"
   65   PRINT:PRINT
   70   FOR J=1 TO N: NEXT
   80   PRINT "CHANGE THE VALUES OF N IN THE FOR-NEXT LOOP"
   85   PRINT:PRINT:PRINT:PRINT
   90   FOR J=1 TO N: NEXT
   100  PRINT "IF YOU WISH TO STOP THIS DISPLAY"
   105  PRINT:PRINT
   110  FOR J=1 TO N: NEXT
   120  PRINT "HOLD DOWN 'CTRL' KEY AND PRESS 'C'"
   130  FOR J=1 TO N: NEXT
   140  GOTO 20
   ```

2. Make certain that you understand this program and can explain it to your teacher.

PRACTICE 18

Counting Programs Using IF-THEN and FOR-NEXT

1. Using IF-THEN, write a program to count 5's from 50 to 5.
   a. Written vertically
   b. Written horizontally
2. *Do not* type NEW (that is, save the program above).
3. Using FOR-NEXT, write a program to count to 50 by 5's written horizontally.
   Note: Start your second program at Line 100. That is, type Line 100 as follows: 100 PRINT : PRINT (Of course, this is to insert two spaces between your outputs.)
4. How many program lines (excluding Line 100) did it take using FOR-NEXT? _____
   How many using IF-THEN? _____
5. What can you conclude from this task?

PRACTICE 19

Using IF-THEN and FOR-NEXT Statements

1. Using IF-THEN, write a program to generate all the even numbers between 11 and 51 from smallest to the largest (that is, 12, 14, 16, and so forth).
2. *Do not* type NEW.
3. Using FOR-NEXT, write a program that generates the same numbers and PRINT them horizontally. (*Note:* Start at Line 100. Type Line 100 as → 100 PRINT : PRINT and your next line should be 110.)
4. Type NEW and enter.
5. Using IF-THEN, write a program to generate all even numbers between 11 and 51 from largest to the smallest.
6. Do the same using FOR-NEXT.

PART 11

Reading Data

What You Will Learn

1. To explain the purpose and use of the key words READ, DATA, RESTORE.

2. To compare the three different ways you have learned to input data into the Apple II.

3. To write, enter, and run programs using READ-DATA and READ-RESTORE key words.

READ-DATA

READ-DATA statements are much more efficient than INPUT or LET statements when you have lots of data to input.

Ways of Inputting Data to the Computer
(i.e., Ways We've Learned So Far)

10 LET A = 5	10 INPUT A	10 DATA ⑤↓
		20 READ A
BUILT-IN	**FROM KEYBOARD**	**READ-DATA COMBINATION**

Ways of Inputting Data to the Computer

STATEMENT   FUNCTION

- 1∅ LET A = 5   • LET statement builds value into the program.
  OR
- 1∅ INPUT A   • INPUT statement allows you to enter
  OR   data through the keyboard.
- 1∅ DATA ⑤   • DATA statement contains the value (5), which
                                              will be stored in a specified variable.
  2∅ READ A   • READ statement names the variables in
                                              which the values are to be stored.

NOTES: Data lines can be read only by READ statements.
          The READ-DATA work together to input data to the computer.

READ-DATA Example

5 REM*READ — DATA EXAMPLE*

(DATA STATEMENT) → 1Ø DATA ①, ②, ③, ④, ⑤

(READ STATEMENT) → 2Ø READ A, B, C, D, E

(PRINT STATEMENT) → 3Ø PRINT A, B, C, D, E

NOTES:
- Each piece of data must be read by a READ statement.
- Each READ statement can read a number of pieces of data if each variable is separated by a comma.
- Data lines can only be used by READ statements.

Exercise 11-1 (Reading Data)

Type and enter.
```
10 DATA 1, 2, 3, 4, 5
20 READ A, B, C, D, E
30 PRINT A, B, C, D, E
```

Type RUN and press RETURN .
```
1        2        3
4        5
```

NOTES:
- **The display shows that all five pieces of data in Line 10 were read by Line 20, assigned letters A through E, and printed by Line 30.**
- **Data lines are always read left to right by READ statements.**

READ-DATA Summary (Key Words)

DATA
- Key word that lets you store data inside your program to be accessed (read) by READ statements.
  - Data items will be read sequentially starting with the first item in the first DATA statement and ending with the last item in the last DATA statement.
  - Items in data list may be string or numeric constants.
  - If string values include leading blanks, colons, or commas, you must enclose these values in quotes.
  - DATA statements must match up with the variable types in the corresponding READ statement.
  - DATA statements may appear anywhere it is convenient in a program.

- EXAMPLE:

  10 DATA "JONES, A.B.", "SMITH, R.J."
  20 DATA LEEDS MIDDLE SCHOOL, COMPUTERS
  30 DATA 125, 250, 750, 1000

  Note: Quotes used here because of commas

READ-DATA Summary (Key Words)

READ

- Key word that instructs the computer to read a value from a DATA statement and assign that value to the specified variable.
  - The first time a READ statement is executed, the first value in the first DATA statement is used; the second time, the second value in the DATA statement is used. When all the items in the first DATA statement are used (READ), the next READ will use the first value in the second DATA statement, and so on.
  - An out-of-data error occurs if there are more attempts to READ than there are data items.

- EXAMPLE:

  40 READ A$, B$, C$, D$, A, B, C, D

  (Note that there are eight READ variables and eight DATA items on previous page for program Lines 10, 20, and 30)

Assignment 11-1

1. Type and enter the following program:
   10 PRINT "NAME", "GRADE"
   20 READ A$
   30 IF A$ = "END" THEN PRINT "END OF LIST": END
   40 READ G
   50 IF G < 75 THEN PRINT A$, G
   60 GOTO 20
   70 DATA "GRAY, BILL", 95, "JONES, A.B.", 65
   80 DATA "JONES, A.C.", 100, "SMITH, R.L.", 70
   90 DATA "EPPS, S.W.", 60, "WELLS, DAVE", 100, END

2. Predict the output of the program.

3. Why were quotes used in the DATA statements?

4. RUN the program and record the results.

RESTORE

- Key word that causes the next READ statement executed to start over with the first DATA statement.
  - This lets your program reuse the same data lines.
  - Sometimes it is necessary to READ the same data more than once without having to run the complete program again; therefore, RESTORE is used.
  - Whenever the program comes to RESTORE, all data lines are restored to their original unread condition, both those lines that have been READ and those that have not been READ. This allows all data to be available for reading again, starting with the first data item in the first data line.

NOTE! Remember that each piece of data in a data line can only be read once each time the program is RUN. The next time a READ statement requests a piece of data, it will READ the next piece of data in the data line, or, if data on that line are all used up, it will go to the next data line and start reading it. Therefore, the RESTORE statement is needed if the same data is to be READ more than once in the same program.

Illustration of the READ-RESTORE Feature

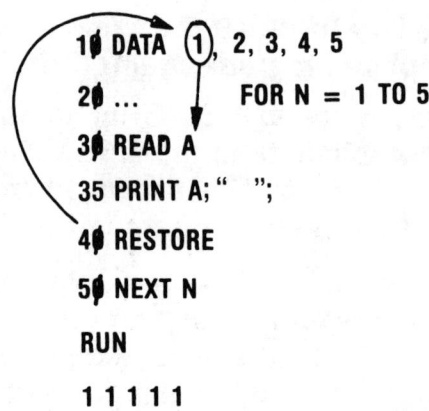

```
10 DATA 1, 2, 3, 4, 5
20 ...           FOR N = 1 TO 5
30 READ A
35 PRINT A; " ";
40 RESTORE
50 NEXT N
RUN
1 1 1 1 1
```

NOTE:
- **RESTORE caused data Line 10 to be restored to its original unread condition, making all data available for reading again.**
- **Since there is only one read variable, A, it starts with the first piece of data, 1, in this case.**

Exercise 11-2 (READ-RESTORE Data in a FOR-NEXT Loop)

YOUR ACTION	DISPLAY	
1. Type and enter.	10 DATA 1, 2, 3, 4, 5 20 FOR N = 1 TO 5 30 READ A 40 PRINT A ; " "; 50 NEXT N	
2. Type RUN and press **RETURN**.	1 2 3 4 5	
3. Insert Line 35. (Type and enter)	35 RESTORE	**Restores Data Line to Its Original Unread Condition**
4. Type RUN and press **RETURN**.	1 1 1 1 1	**Therefore Computer Reads First Data Item Over and Over**

READ-DATA SUMMARY

- **READ-DATA**
  — Key words used to input lots of data to the computer.
- **RESTORE**
  — Key word used to restore (put back) data so it can be used again.
- **Data lines can be read only by READ statements.**
  — If more than one piece of data is placed on a data line, they must be separated by commas.
  Each piece of data must be read by a READ statement.
- **Data lines are read from left to right by READ statements.**
  — Data lines can be placed anywhere in a program.
- **READ-DATA statements are extremely common.**
  — RESTORE is used less often.

PRACTICE 20

READ-DATA

1. Type and enter the following program:
   ```
   5  HOME
   10 PRINT "NAME", "GRADE"
   20 READ A$
   30 IF A$ = "END" THEN PRINT "END OF LIST":END
   40 READ G
   50 IF G > 75 PRINT A$, G
   60 GOTO 20
   70 DATA "GRAY,BILL", 95,"JONES, A.B.", 65
   80 DATA "JONES,A.C.", 100, "SMITH, R.L.", 70
   90 DATA "EPPS, S.W.", 60, "WELLS, DAVE", 100, END
   ```
2. Predict the output of the program.
3. Why were quotes used in the data statements?
4. RUN the program and record the results.

PART 12

Video Display Graphics

What You Will Learn

1. To explain the purpose of key words NORMAL, INVERSE, FLASH, TAB, HTAB, VTAB, GR, COLOR, TEXT, PLOT, HLIN, VLIN.

2. To become familiar with the layout of Apple II display using the Video Display Worksheets.

3. To draw pictures and letters on the screen.

4. To write and run programs using all the concepts learned in this lesson.

NOTE: The Apple II provides the user with an unlimited number of possibilities of graphic application. The student should experiment with graphics. This lesson will introduce the student to some of the basic features of graphics used on Apple II, but we will only "scratch the surface." Students will find out by themselves what other kinds of things can be done with graphics on the Apple II.

Commands — Normal, Inverse, Flash

	Function	How Executed
• Normal	• Sets the video display to the usual white on black.	Normal (immediate)* 10 Normal (deferred)
• Inverse	• Sets the video display to produce black letters on a white background.	Inverse (immediate)* 20 Inverse (deferred)
• Flash	• Sets the video display to flashing characters. It is actually rapidly alternating between normal and inverse.	Flash (immediate)* 30 Flash (deferred)

*Immediate execution of each statement means that the command is executed as soon as it is typed (followed by pressing RETURN).

- Deferred execution refers to commands which are within a program, i.e., which have line numbers. Deferred execution commands are not executed until your program is run.

In-Class Exercise 12-1
(NORMAL, INVERSE, and FLASH)

- Type and enter:

```
5    HOME
10   FOR I = 1 TO 3
20   PRINT
30   NEXT I
40   PRINT "THIS IS NORMAL TEXT"
50   FOR I = 1 TO 3
70   PRINT
80   NEXT I
85   FOR I = 1 TO 2000: NEXT
90   INVERSE
100  PRINT "THIS IS INVERSE TEXT (BLACK ON WHITE)"
110  NORMAL
115  FOR I = 1 TO 2000: NEXT
120  FOR I = 1 TO 3
130  PRINT
140  NEXT I
150  FLASH
160  PRINT "AND THIS IS FLASHING TEXT"
170  NORMAL
175  FOR I = 1 TO 5000: NEXT
180  FOR I = 1 TO 3
190  PRINT
200  NEXT I
210  PRINT "FLASHING IS NICE FOR " ;: FLASH : PRINT
     "HIGHLIGHTING" ;: NORMAL : PRINT " THINGS"
```

- Now run the program several times.

In-Class Exercise 12-1 (Questions)

1. Line 5 _____ the screen.

2. Line 85 is a _____ so that the output will remain on the screen for a while.

3. Lines 10-30 cause _____ blank lines to be printed on the screen.

4. Which line changes the screen output to a black on white display?

5. Predict what would happen by erasing line 110. Try it.
   (Type 110 and RETURN * and then run the program.)

*This will erase line 110.

- PRINT TAB (n)
  — Moves the cursor to the position that is (n) printing positions from left margin. Example: PRINT TAB (20) "TABBED 20."
  — Where (n) must be in the range 1 to 255.
  — If n = 0, then TAB (0) puts cursor into position 256. (See illustration on page 164.)
  — TAB (n) moves cursor to the right only.
  — TAB (n) for (n) = 1 to 40 corresponds to the 40 columns on the display, but since TAB will tab past the length of the screen and "wrap around" to the next line, (n) can have value up to 255.

- HTAB n
  — HTAB works like TAB except that it is not used within a PRINT statement (i.e., you can TAB horizontally with HTAB if you don't want to use a PRINT statement). See page 166.
  — HTAB can cause printing to begin to the left or right of the current printing position.

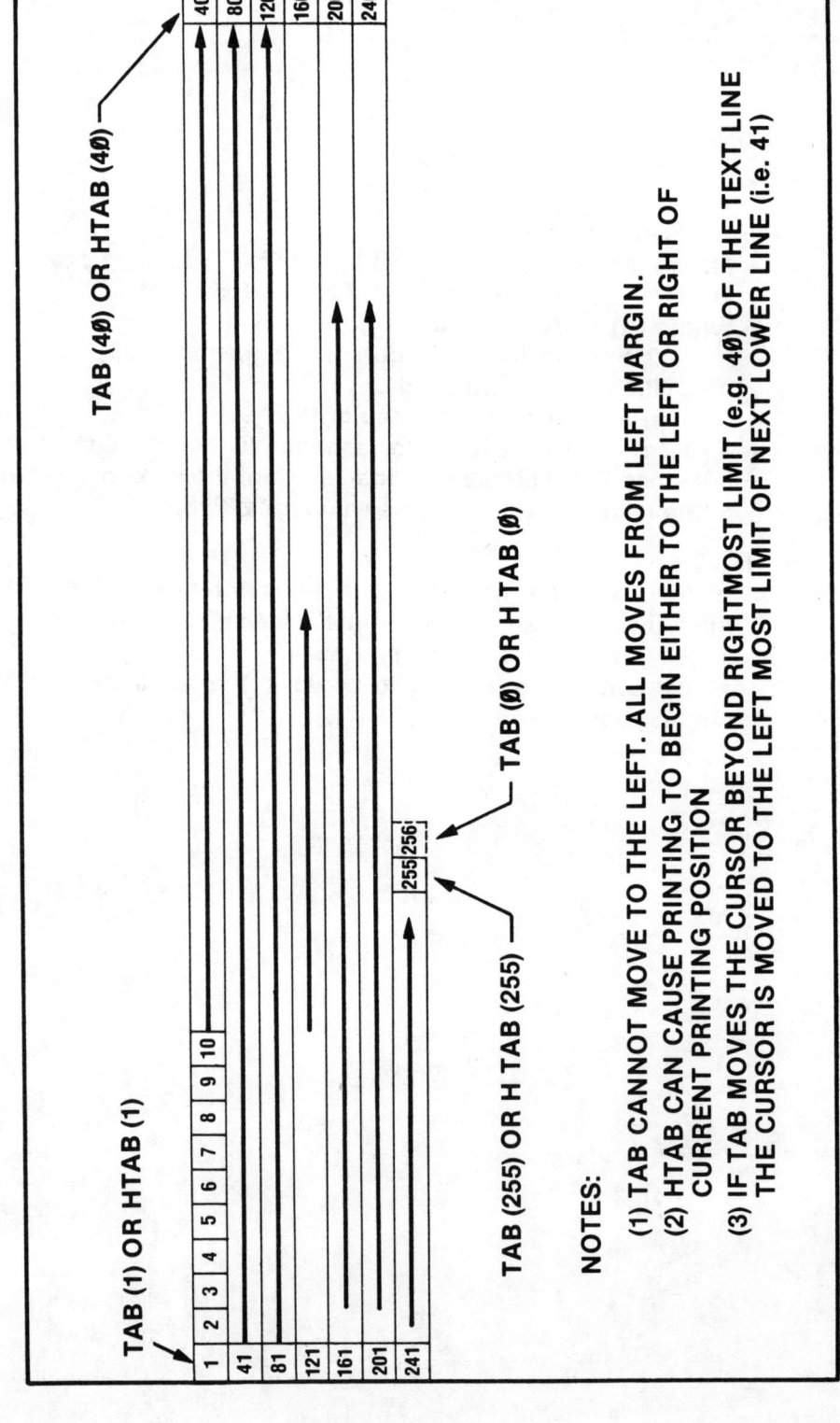

TAB Example

• YOUR ACTION	DISPLAY

1. Type and enter the program shown. ⟶

```
 5 HOME
10 PRINT TAB (1) "TABBED 1": PRINT
20 PRINT TAB (5) "TABBED 5": PRINT
30 PRINT TAB (10) "TABBED 10": PRINT
40 PRINT TAB (20) "TABBED 20": PRINT
50 PRINT TAB (30) "TABBED 30": PRINT
60 PRINT TAB (40) "TABBED 40": PRINT
70 PRINT TAB (255) "TABBED 255"
```

2. RUN the program. (Note that TAB tells the computer where to *start* printing for each print statement.)

```
TABBED 1
   TABBED 5
      TABBED 10
            TABBED 20
                      TABBED 30
ABBED 40
    TABBED 255
```

3. Type and enter the program lines shown. ⟶

```
100 HOME
110 PRINT TAB(0) "TABBED 0"

                TABBED 0
                   ↑
            (Print position 256)
```

4. RUN 100
(Note that TAB (0) starts printing in print positon 256. If you don't believe me count them.)

HTAB Example

• **YOUR ACTION**   **DISPLAY**

1. **Type and enter the program shown.** →

   ```
   10 HOME
   20 HTAB 1:PRINT"TABBED 1":PRINT
   30 HTAB 5:PRINT"TABBED 5": PRINT
   40 HTAB 10:PRINT"TABBED 10":PRINT
   50 HTAB 20:PRINT"TABBED 20":PRINT
   60 HTAB 30:PRINT"TABBED 30":PRINT
   70 HTAB 40:PRINT"TABBED 40":PRINT
   80 HTAB 255:PRINT"TABBED 255":1
   ```

2. **RUN the program. (It looked the same as before when you used TAB, and it should!)**

   ```
   TABBED 1
    TABBED 5
       TABBED 10
              TABBED 20
                        TABBED 30
                                          T
   ABBED 40
     TABBED 255
   ```

TAB and HTAB Examples

YOUR ACTION	DISPLAY
1. Type and enter. →	10 PRINT TAB (20) "YOUR NAME" 20 PRINT TAB (20) "YOUR ADDRESS" 30 PRINT TAB (20) "YOUR TELEPHONE NO."
2. Type RUN and press RETURN. (Sample)	AUBREY JONES 914 E. SEDGWICK ST. 123-4567
3. Type and enter. →	40 HTAB 20 50 PRINT "PHILADELPHIA"
4. Type RUN and press RETURN. (Note that TAB (20) and HTAB 20 give the same results.)	AUBREY JONES 914 E. SEDGWICK ST. 123-4567 PHILADELPHIA

Apple II
Video Display Worksheet For TAB, HTAB & VTAB Functions

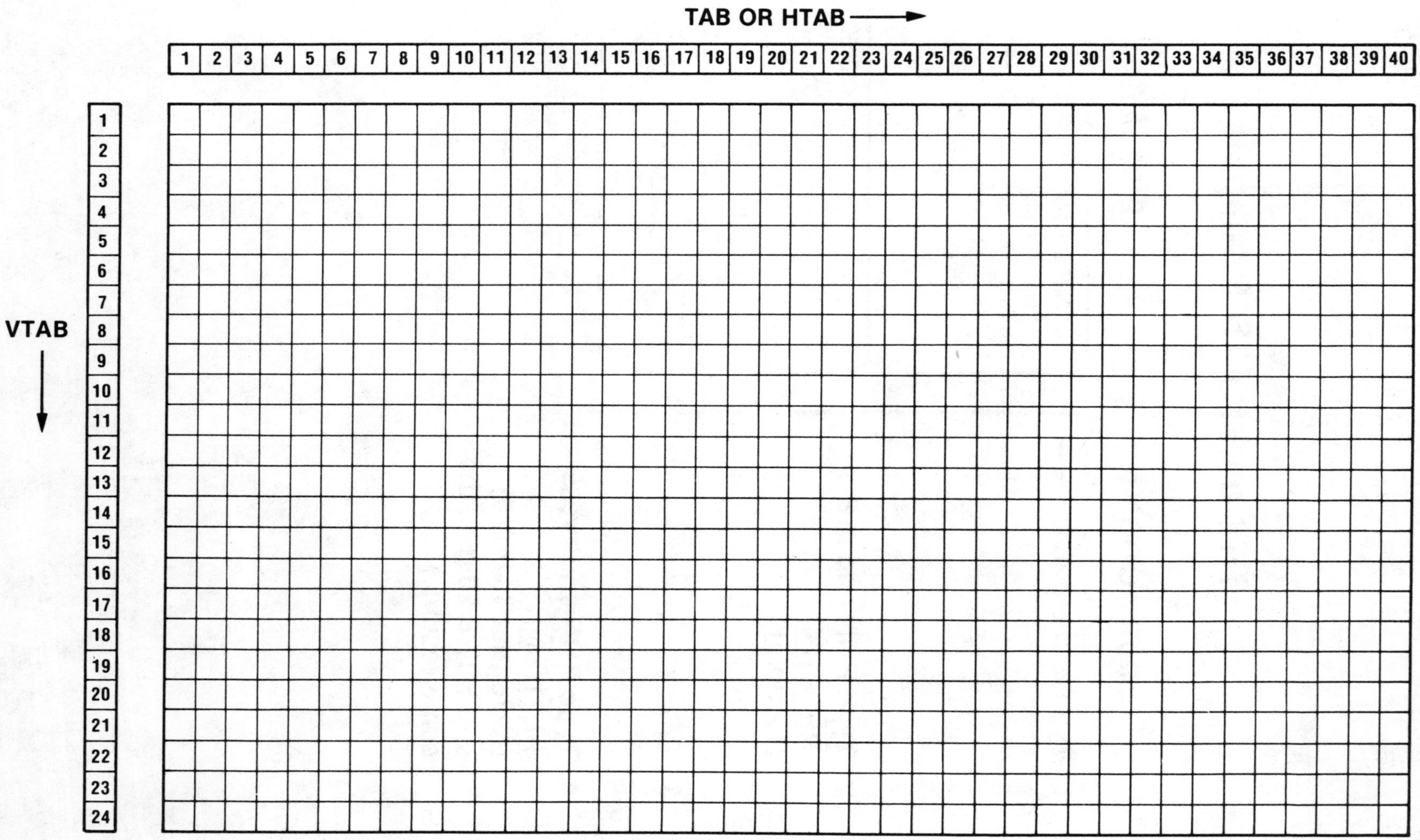

- **VTAB n**
  — Permits you to print on a particular line.
  — Where n must be in the range 1 to 24.
  — If n = 0, VTAB will give you ? illegal quantity error.
  — Not used within PRINT statement.
  — Uses absolute moves, relative only to the top and bottom of the screen.
  (That is, it just moves cursor "up" or "down" without regard to text or graphics mode.)

- **Example:**
  NEW
  10 HOME
  20 FOR K = 1 to 24
  30 VTAB K
  40 PRINT K
  50 NEXT K

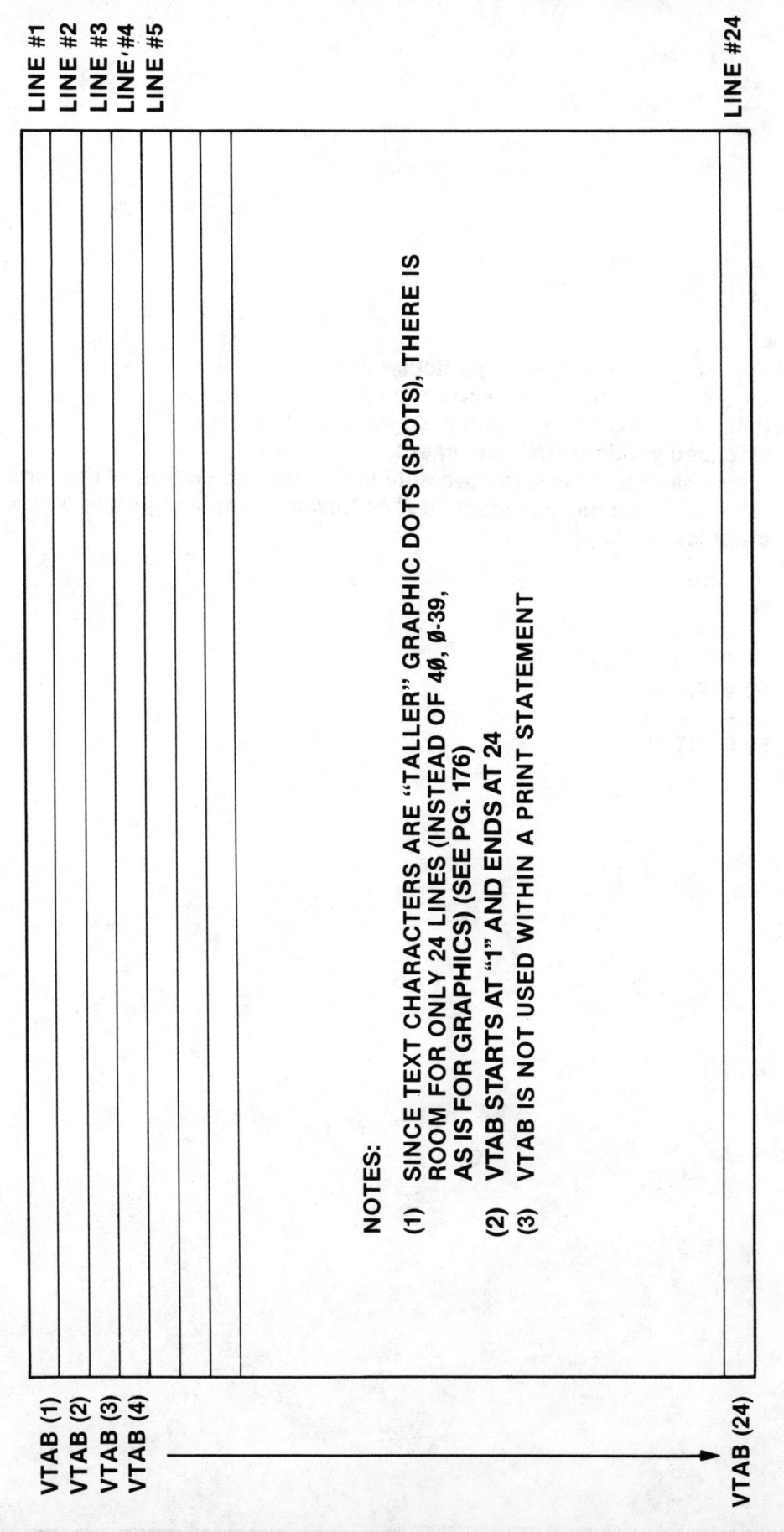

VTAB Example

YOUR ACTION

1. Type & enter program as shown. ⟶

2. RUN the program. (Note difference between VTAB, HTAB, and TAB.)

3. Change lines 20, 40, and 50 as shown. (Do *not* type NEW or change other lines.)

4. RUN the program. (Now you have a combination to HTAB and VTAB. Can you think of ways of using the TAB statement for formatting your output?)

DISPLAY

```
10 HOME
20 VTAB 3:PRINT"VTABBED 3"
30 VTAB 5:PRINT"VTABBED 5"
40 VTAB 10:PRINT"VTABBED 10"
50 VTAB 20:PRINT"VTABBED 20"
```

```
VTABBED 3
VTABBED 5

VTABBED 10


VTABBED 20

]■
```

```
20 VTAB3:HTAB 10:PRINT"VTAB 3 & HTAB 10"
40 VTAB 10:HTAB 15:PRINT"VTAB 10 & HTAB 15"
50 VTAB 23 HTAB 20:PRINT"VTAB 23 & HTAB 20"
```

```
            VTAB 3 & HTAB 10

VTABBED 5

                 VTAB 10 & HTAB 15

VTABBED 20


                    VTAB 23 & HTAB 20
```

In-Class Exercise 12-2

1. Type, enter, and RUN the following program:

   ```
   5 HOME
   10 PRINT TAB (15) "TAB DEMO"
   20 VTAB 10: HTAB 10
   30 PRINT "THIS IS AN EXAMPLE"
   40 VTAB 15:HTAB 18
   50 PRINT "OF"
   60 VTAB 20:HTAB 5
   70 PRINT "USING VTAB & HTAB FOR FORMATTING"
   ```

2. RUN the program several times. Analyze the program and make certain you understand it.

3. Experiment with VTAB, HTAB, and TAB (if you have the time).

TAB Function — Summary

- Used to set up your output format.
- TAB (n) moves the cursor to the specified position that is line (n) printing positions from the left margin.
- HTAB n works like TAB but causes printing to begin either to the left or to the right of current printing position.
  — n must be in the range from 1 to 255.
- VTAB n permits you to print on a particular line.
  — n must be in the range from 1 to 24.
- TAB must be used within a PRINT statement whereas VTAB and HTAB are not used within PRINT statement.
- VTAB and HTAB can be used within a program or in the immediate mode (i.e., no line number) whereas TAB must be used within a program (i.e., it needs line numbers).

Applesoft Graphics

Notes:

- This lesson assumes a black and white monitor is used. If you are using a color monitor refer to the Applesoft manual for additional information.
- To use graphics on the screen, type the following command: GR
- To get back to the text mode, use the following command: TEXT
- When you use the GR command, most of the screen is used for graphics except for four (4) lines at the bottom which are used for TEXT.
- To clear the screen in graphics mode, use the following command: GR

Apple II
Video Display Layout Showing X, Y, Coordinates

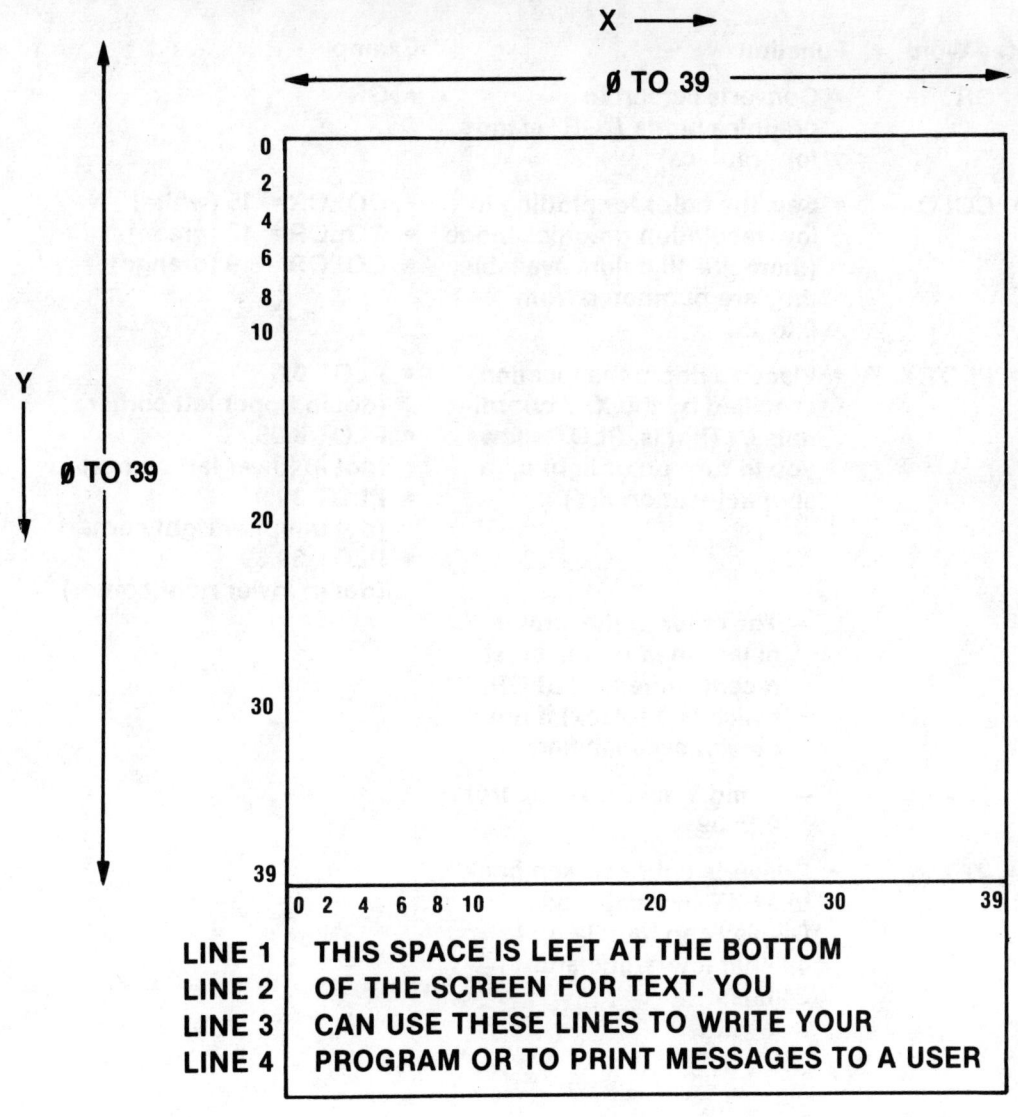

Graphic Commands — GR, COLOR, PLOT, TEXT

Key Word	Function	Example
• GR	• Converts screen to graphics mode ("GR" stands for graphics)	• GR
• COLOR	• Sets the color for plotting in low-resolution graphics mode (there are 16 colors available; they are numbered from 0 to 15)	• COLOR = 15 (white) • COLOR = 12 (green) • COLOR = 9 (orange)
• PLOT X, Y	• Places a dot at the location specified by the X, Y coordinates. (That is, PLOT allows you to turn on or light up a spot at location X,Y)	• PLOT 0,0 (dot in upper left corner) • PLOT 0,39 (dot in lower left corner) • PLOT 39,0 (dot in upper right corner) • PLOT 39,39 (dot in lower right corner)
	— The color of the spot is determined by the most recent value of COLOR, which is 0 (black) if not previously specified	
	— X and Y values range from 0 to 39	
• TEXT	• Converts entire screen back to TEXT (words) mode. Display can handle up to 40 characters/line and 24 lines.	

Apple II
Video Display Worksheet for Graphics (GR) Mode

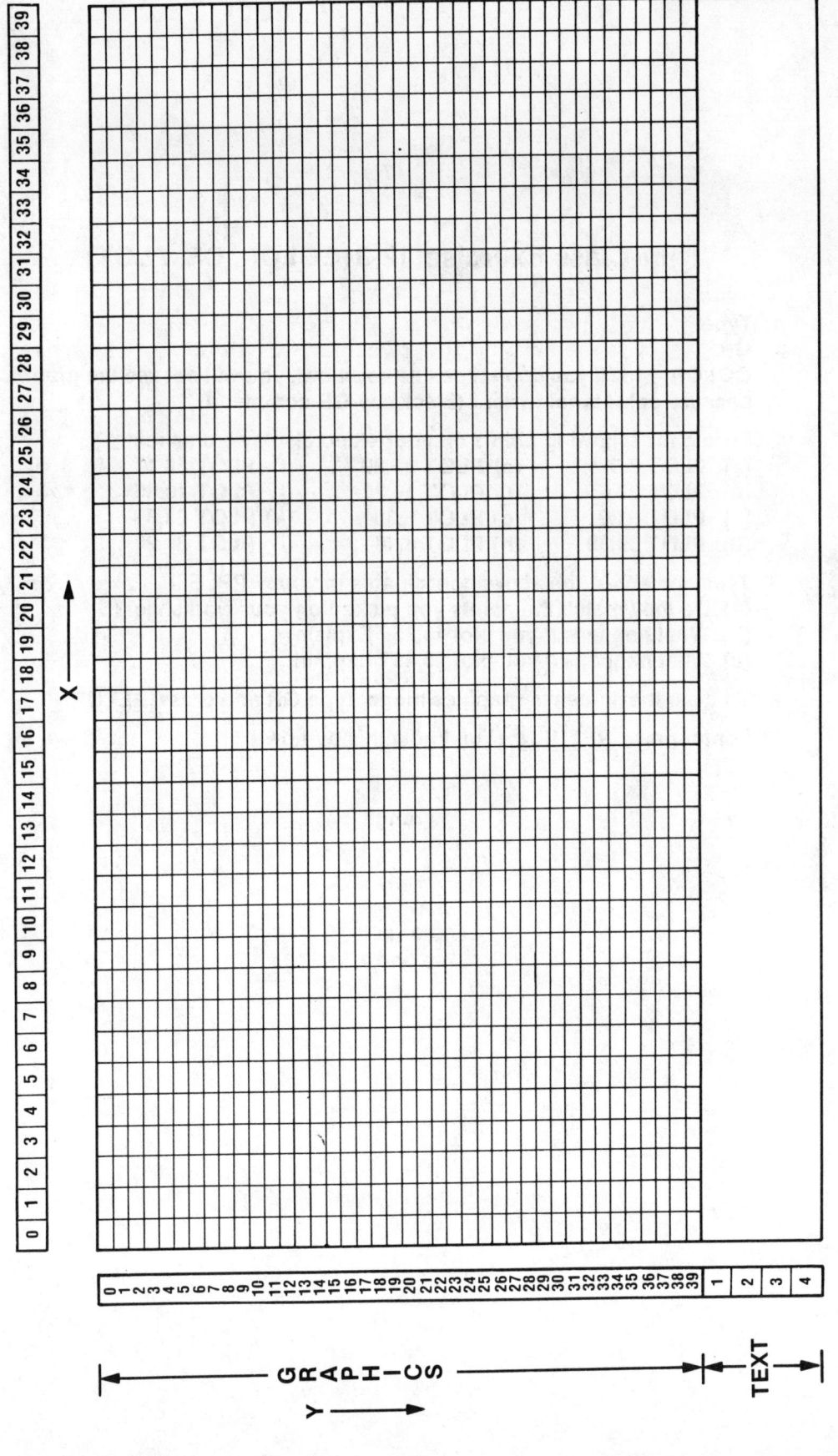

In-Class Exercise 12-3 (COLOR, GR, PLOT)

1. Type:
   GR
   COLOR = 15 (If you don't type this key word, you will not see the graphics because color is set to zero (black) by GR command)

2. Locate the following points on your video display worksheet:
(a) PLOT 9,9	(e) PLOT 20,20	(i) PLOT 36,10
(b) PLOT 39,0	(f) PLOT 10,20	(j) PLOT 10,36
(c) PLOT 0,39	(g) PLOT 6,36	(k) PLOT 28,38
(d) PLOT 39,39	(h) PLOT 8,18	(l) PLOT 38,28

3. Type and enter* the above coordinates in your APPLE II
   (a) Do they match the points you picked on your worksheet?
   (b) What happens if you plot 13,75? Explain.
   (c) What happens if you plot 20,45? Explain.

4. To clear the screen in graphics mode, type GR and press RETURN.

*To enter press RETURN (You know this by now!)

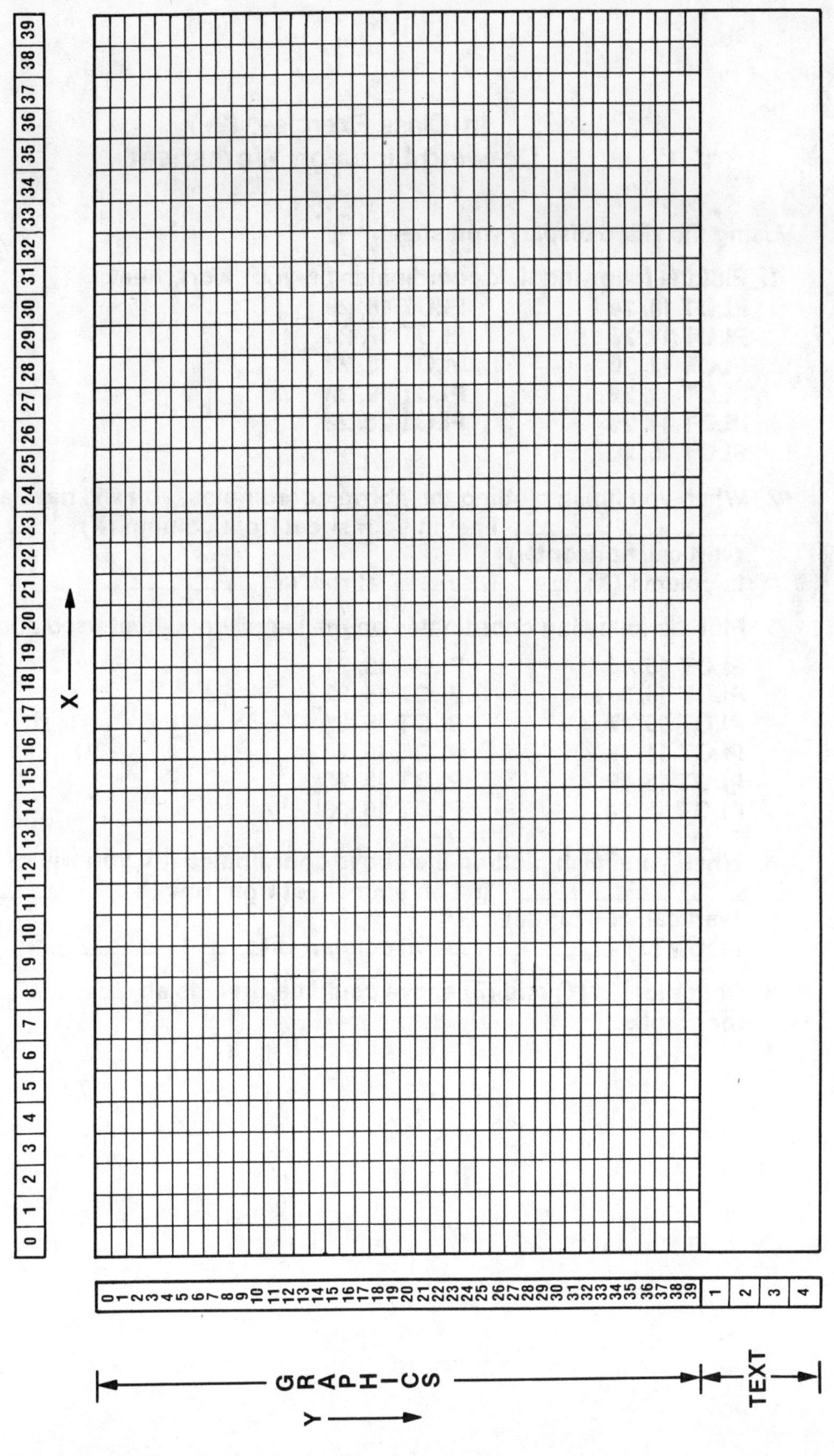

In-Class Exercise 12-4
Drawing Lines on Worksheet

Using the video display worksheet:

1. Plot the following X, Y coordinates on your worksheet:

    PLOT 10, 20   PLOT 16, 20
    PLOT 11, 20   PLOT 17, 20
    PLOT 12, 20   PLOT 18, 20
    PLOT 13, 20   PLOT 19, 20
    PLOT 14, 20   PLOT 20, 20
    PLOT 15, 20

2. When you finish plotting the above coordinates, you will have a _____ line on your sheet from column (X) _____
   (vertical, horizontal)
   to column (X) _____ at row (Y) _____.

3. Plot the following coordinates on the same worksheet used above:

    PLOT 15, 15   PLOT 15, 21
    PLOT 15, 16   PLOT 15, 22
    PLOT 15, 17   PLOT 15, 23
    PLOT 15, 18   PLOT 15, 24
    PLOT 15, 19   PLOT 15, 25
    PLOT 15, 20   PLOT 15, 26

4. When you finish plotting the above coordinates (3), you will have a _____ line on your sheet from row (Y) _____
   (vertical, horizontal)
   to row (Y) _____ at column (X) _____.

5. Both plots in (1) and (3) above could be used as an _____ axis for graphs.

In-Class Exercise 12-5
Drawing Lines on Apple II (The Hard Way)

1. **Horizontal lines**
   (a) Set color = 15 and enter information below (don't forget to press RETURN after each line).
   COLOR = 15
   PLOT 10, 20   PLOT 16, 20
   PLOT 11, 20   PLOT 17, 20
   PLOT 12, 20   PLOT 18, 20
   PLOT 13, 20   PLOT 19, 20
   PLOT 14, 20   PLOT 20, 20
   PLOT 15, 20

   (b) What happened? _____

2. **Vertical Lines**
   (a) Set color = 15 and enter information below (don't forget to press RETURN).
   COLOR = 15
   PLOT 15, 15   PLOT 15, 21
   PLOT 15, 16   PLOT 15, 22
   PLOT 15, 17   PLOT 15, 23
   PLOT 15, 18   PLOT 15, 24
   PLOT 15, 19   PLOT 15, 25
   PLOT 15, 20   PLOT 15, 26

   (b) What happened? _____

3. Make up some coordinates on your own and try it!

Summary and Assignment 12-1
GR, COLOR, PLOT, TEXT

Summary

1. Screen is divided into 40 vertical columns and 40 horizontal rows.
   — X is the horizontal coordinate counting across from the left-hand side of the screen. X coordinate goes from 0 to 39.
   — Y is the vertical coordinate counting from the top of the screen. Y coordinate goes from 0 to 39.

2. PLOT X,Y lights up a spot on the screen.
   — The X and Y coordinates for graphics go from 0 to 39.
   — If you try to plot a point outside the range (e.g., PLOT 15, 75), you get the message "? ILLEGAL QUANTITY ERROR."
   — If you use negative values in a PLOT command (e.g., PLOT −15, −30), you will also get "? ILLEGAL QUANTITY ERROR" message.
   — Although the highest number you can use with the "Y" coordinate is "47," don't do it! A "Y" coordinate in the range 40 to 47 will just give you peculiar characters in the text area. (The last four lines at the bottom of the screen).

3. Assignment 12-1
   Experiment with PLOT command on your own time until you feel comfortable with it.

In-Class Exercise 12-6
Drawing Lines on Apple II (The Easy Way)

1. **Horizontal Lines**
   (a) Type and enter the following program:
   COLOR = 15
   HLIN 0, 39 at 20
   RETURN

   (b) What happened? _____

   (c) How many PLOT statements would you need to type to draw the above line the hard way? _____

2. **Vertical Line**
   (a) Type and enter the following program:
   COLOR = 15
   VLIN 0, 39 at 20
   RETURN

   (b) What happened? _____

3. Try some other examples. Play with HLIN and VLIN until you feel comfortable using these key words to draw lines.

4. Can you think of other things you can draw using the VLIN and HLIN commands? (Try some, if you have the time.)

Summary of Graphing Lines

- HLIN A*, B* AT C* will place a horizontal line from X coordinate A* to X coordinate B* at Y coordinate C*.
- VLIN D*, E* AT F* will place a vertical line from Y coordinate D* to Y coordinate E* at X coordinate F*.

*In an actual example, each of these letters would be replaced with a number between 0 and 39.

- Type and enter:

```
10   GR
20   COLOR = 15
30   HLIN 10,12 AT 1
40   HLIN 10,12 AT 3
50   VLIN 1,6 AT 10
60   VLIN 1,6 AT 12
80   HLIN 15,17 AT 7
90   HLIN 15,17 AT 9
100  VLIN 7,12 AT 15
110  VLIN 7,9 AT 17
130  HLIN 18,20 AT 14
140  HLIN 18,20 AT 16
150  VLIN 14,19 AT 18
160  VLIN 14,16 AT 20
180  VLIN 21,26 AT 22
190  HLIN 22,24 AT 26
210  VLIN 28,33 AT 27
220  HLIN 27,29 AT 28
230  HLIN 27,29 AT 30
240  HLIN 27,29 AT 33
260  HOME
270  INVERSE: PRINT "VOILA! APPLE GRAPHICS."
280  NORMAL
```

- Now RUN the program several times.

In-Class Exercise 12-7

Match the letter printed in Column I with the line numbers in Column II.

I	II
1. A _____	a. 210-240
2. P _____	b. 30-60
3. L _____	c. 180-190
4. E _____	d. 80-110

5. Change the color value in line 20 to 0 (Color = 0). Before running the program, predict what will happen.

6. Write a program to print the first letter of your name.

PRACTICE 21

Graphics

1. Write a program that will do the following:
   a. Draw a horizontal line across the top of the screen (Line Ø).
   b. Add the necessary steps to your program to draw a vertical line down the middle of the screen.
   c. Add the necessary steps to your program to draw a horizontal line across the bottom of the screen (last line of the display).
   d. Add the necessary steps to draw a vertical line on the far left side of the display.
   e. Add the necessary steps to draw a vertical line to the far right side of the display.
   f. Enter and RUN your program.

Display should look like this after part (E).

PART 13

Arrays

What You Will Learn

1. To explain the purpose of using arrays.

2. To set up one- and two-dimensional numeric arrays.

3. To explain the purpose and use of the terms DIM, A(3), A(2,3), DIM A(10), DIM DB(7,5).

4. To develop, enter, and run programs using numeric arrays.

Arrays

A. What is an array?
- An array is a lineup, an arrangement, or an orderly grouping of things.

B. Why use an array?
- Use it when we wish to have more variables available in a program.
  — Although the Applesoft BASIC permits the use of approximately 900 variables for numerics, sometimes thousands of variables are required for storing and retrieving many pieces of data.
  — The array allows you to arrange your data so that it can be stored and retrieved easily.

One-Dimensional Array — Illustration

SIX-ELEMENT ARRAY — NAMED A*   **SIX-ELEMENT ARRAY — NAMED B***

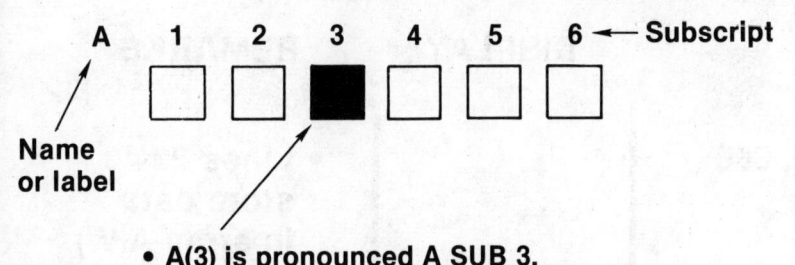
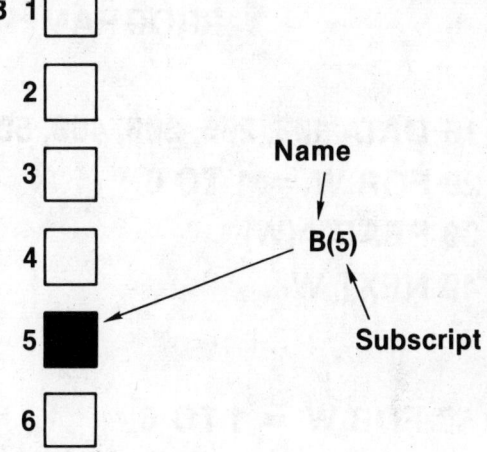

- A(3) is pronounced A SUB 3.
  — A(3) represents the third cell or box in the array (lineup).
  — Data stored in this cell would be addressed by the label A(3).
  — Suppose data were stored in the sixth cell: A(6)? (You got it!)

- B(5) represents the fifth cell in the array where data can be stored and retrieved.

*A and B are optional names. Any valid variable name can be used to name an array in Applesoft BASIC.

One-Dimensional Array — Program Example

PROGRAM	DISPLAY	REMARKS
1Ø DATA 1ØØ, 2ØØ, 3ØØ, 4ØØ, 5ØØ, 6ØØ 2Ø FOR W = 1 TO 6 3Ø READ A(W) 4Ø NEXT W		• Lines 2Ø-4Ø store data in array A(W)
5Ø FOR W = 1 TO 6 6Ø PRINT W, A(W) 7Ø NEXT W RUN	1 1ØØ 2 2ØØ 3 3ØØ 4 4ØØ 5 5ØØ 6 6ØØ	• Lines 5Ø-7Ø retrieve data from array A(W)

One-Dimensional Array — Program Example (Con't)

```
           ARRAY
           CONTENTS

           A(W)
           A(1) ⟶ 100
           A(2) ⟶ 200
           A(3) ⟶ 300
           A(4) ⟶ 400
           A(5) ⟶ 500
           A(6) ⟶ 600
```

Above is an illustration of what happens after data are stored in array A(W). Note that in location A(1), the first data element (100) is stored. In location A(2), the second data element (200) is stored, and so on until the sixth data element (600) is stored in location A(6). Remember that line 10 of the program contained the data elements that were read using lines 20 through 40.

Two-Dimensional Array — Illustration

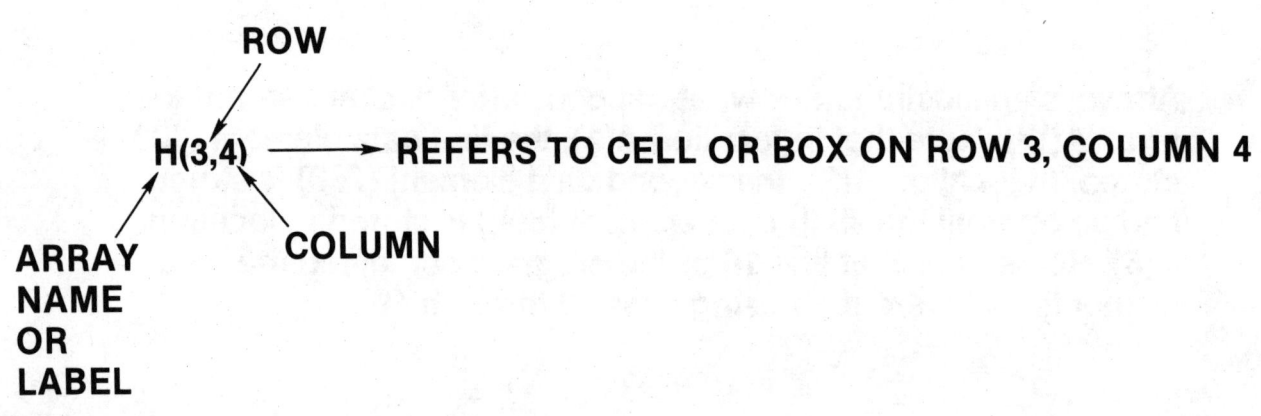

**36 ELEMENT ARRAY (MATRIX)
(NAMED H)**

H(3,4) → REFERS TO CELL OR BOX ON ROW 3, COLUMN 4

ARRAY NAME OR LABEL

In-Class Exercise 13-1

(Fill in the Blanks Using the Matrix)

LABEL	ROW	COLUMN	CONTENTS
H(1,1)	___	___	___
H(4,5)	___	___	___
H(3,3)	___	___	___
H(2,3)	___	___	___
H(6,6)	___	___	___
H(1,6)	___	___	___
H(2,4)	___	___	___
H(4,4)	___	___	___

DIM Statement

- **DIM** - Lets you set the depth (number of elements allowed per dimension)
  — If no DIM statement is used, a depth of 11 (subscripts 0-10) is allowed for each dimension of each array used.
  — DIM statements may be placed anywhere in your program.

- **EXAMPLE**

     10   DIM   A(6),   B(2,3),   C(21)
                   ↑   ↑   ↑

Sets a one-dimension array A with 6 elements
A(0) — A(5)
or
A(1) — A(6)*

Sets a two-dimension array B with 3 ROWS (numbered 0-2) and 4 COLUMNS (numbered 0-3)

Sets a one-dimension array with 21 elements
A(0) — A(20) or A(1) — A(21)*

*If A(0) is not used

Checkbook Array Example

- **Consider the following table of checkbook information:**

Check #	Date Written	Amount
100	6/5/81	$ 15.50
101	6/7/81	25.00
102	6/15/81	145.00
103	6/22/81	65.00
104	6/30/81	211.00
105	6/30/81	79.50

- **Note that every item in the table may be specified by reference to two numbers: the row number and the column number. For example, (Row 3, Column 3) refers to the amount $145.00.**

- **The above table can be set up in a 6 × 3 array or matrix (see next page).**

Checkbook Array Example (Con't)

CK	1	2	3
1	100	60581	15.50
2	101	60781	25.00
3	102	61581	145.00
4	103	62281	65.00
5	104	63081	211.00
6	105	63081	79.50

6 × 3 MATRIX (ARRAY) — NAMED CK

NOTES:

1. Data recorded in form mm ddyy where mm = month number, dd = day, and yy = last two digits of year.

2. Since CK is a numeric array, alpha-numerical characters such as dashes cannot be stored.

Checkbook Array Example (Con't)

YOUR ACTION	DISPLAY

1. **Setting Up the Array**
   (Lines 10 through 110)

   A. **Let's type and enter Lines 10 through 110 as shown:** →

   (NOTE: Line 10 sets up dimension of array. Lines 20-110 read the values into array CK.)

   NOTE: DIM CK (6, 3) Sets up a 6 × 3 array (excluding zero subscripts) with 6 rows (numbered 1 to 6) and 3 columns (numbered 1 to 3)

2. **Manipulating the Array**
   (Finding the Sum)

   A. **Add lines 120 through 150 to the program as shown:**

   (NOTE: Lines 120-150 add up all the checks written.)

   B. **Type RUN and press RETURN.**

```
10 DIM CK (6,3)
20 FOR ROW = 1 TO 6
30 FOR COL = 1 TO 3
40 READ CK(ROW, COL)
50 NEXT COL, ROW
60 DATA 100, 60581, 15.50
70 DATA 101, 60781, 25.00
80 DATA 102, 61581, 145.00
90 DATA 103, 62281,  65.00
100 DATA 104, 63081, 211.00
110 DATA 105, 63081,  79.50
120 FOR ROW = 1 TO 6
130 SUM = SUM + CK (ROW, 3)
140 NEXT ROW
150 PRINT "TOTAL $"; SUM
```

TOTAL OF CHECKS WRITTEN $541

NOTE: ROW and COL are used for convenience. Remember, however, the computer will only use the first two characters, RO and CO in this example.

Checkbook Array Example (Con't)

YOUR ACTION	DISPLAY

3. Manipulating the Array
   (Print out all checks written
   on a given day)

A. Do not type NEW.

B. Add the following steps to your program:

```
200 INPUT "LIST CHECKS WRITTEN ON (MM DD YY)"; DT
210 PRINT: PRINT "CHECKS WRITTEN ON"; DT; "ARE LISTED BELOW:"
215 PRINT
220 PRINT "CHECK #", "AMOUNT": PRINT
230 FOR ROW = 1 TO 6
240 IF CK (ROW,2) = DT THEN PRINT CK (ROW,1), CK (ROW,3)
250 NEXT
```

C. Type RUN and press `RETURN`.

```
TOTAL OF CHECKS WRITTEN $541
LIST CHECKS WRITTEN ON (MM DDYY)? --
```

D. Enter a date (e.g., 63081 which is 6/30/81).

```
CHECKS WRITTEN ON 63081 ARE LISTED BELOW;

CHECK #      AMOUNT
104          211
105          79.5
```

Assignment 13-1

Read pages 108-111 in the Applesoft Tutorial manual.

Summary

- A2 ≠ A(2)
  - A2 is an ordinary variable
  - A(2) is a subscripted variable
- Any time you have a subscript larger than 10 (depth of 11), you must use a DIM statement.
  - Example:

    10 DIMA (25), B(17, 18)

- One-Dimensional Array

          SUBSCRIPT
  - A(3) is pronounced A SUB 3

  NAME

- Two-Dimensional Array (Matrix)

          ROW
  - H(3,4) refers to cell or box on row 3, column 4

  NAME COLUMN

PRACTICE 22

Arrays

1. Write a program to read the following numbers into an array and then PRINT them out:
   676 150 175 188 190 277 876 976 912 544
2. Change program to find the sum and average of the 10 numbers given.
3. Label the answer: The sum is _____, and the average is _____.

PRACTICE 23

One-Dimensional Array

1. Suppose we had the following results of a quiz given to a class of 10 students:

Student #	1	2	3	4	5	6	7	8	9	10
Student's Grade	75	85	95	87	100	77	83	69	98	88

   a. Using a one-dimensional Array, write a program to find the class average.
   b. Add the necessary program lines to find the highest grade and the lowest grade.
   c. Have the program PRINT : Class Average is _____, Highest Grade is _____ and Lowest Grade is _____.
   d. Enter and RUN each of these programs several times.

PART 14

INT(X), ABS(X) & RND(X) Functions

What You Will Learn

1. To explain the purpose and use of INT(X), ABS(X), and RND(X) functions.

2. To write, run, and analyze programs using the INT(X), ABS(X), and RND(X) functions.

INT(X) Function

- INT(X) or integer function allows you to round off any number, large or small, positive or negative, into a whole number (or integer).
- INT(X) means
  — If X is a positive number, then the largest whole number can be found by chopping off the decimal part.

  Example:

  INT (5.7) = 5

  INT (0.7) = 0

  — If X is a negative number, the largest whole number can be found by moving down to the next lowest whole number (that is, make a negative number more negative).

  Examples:

  INT (−.6) = −1   INT (−3.14) = −4

  INT (−.2) = −1   INT (−7.28) = −8

Exercise 14-1 INT(X)

Graphical Representation

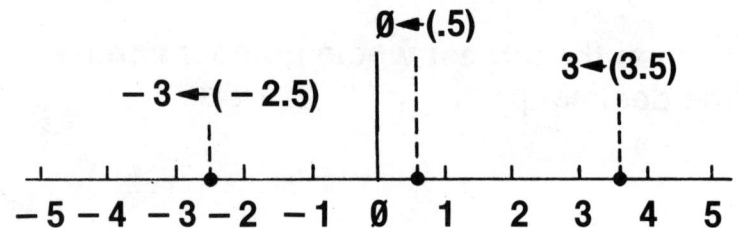

For negative numbers: "Move to next lowest whole number"

For positive numbers: "Chop off decimal part"

X	INT(X)
0.5	_____
−1.7	_____
2.345	_____
−0.8	_____
0	_____
3.1415	_____
76.14	_____
−10.35	_____

INT(X) FUNCTION — ROUNDING $$

YOUR ACTION

1. **Type and enter this program.** →
2. **Now RUN.**

3. **Add Line 15 to program as shown.**
   (Note: In Line 15 we multiply by 100, add .5, take the INT, which is now 667, and then divide 667 by 100. 667/100 is 6.67, which is what we want, two decimal places.)
4. **Now RUN program.**

DISPLAY

10 LET A = 20/3
20 PRINT "$"; A
  $ 6.66667

15 A = INT (100*6.66667+.5)/100

$6.67

Assignment 14-1 INT(X)

1. Type NEW and enter this program for finding the area of a circle:

    10 REM**AREA OF A CIRCLE 3.14159*R∧2**
    20 INPUT "THE RADIUS IS"; R
    30 P = 3.14159
    40 A = P*R∧2
    50 PRINT "THE AREA IS "; A

2. RUN the program several times to make sure it works.

3. Change the program to suppress (chop off) all of the numbers to the right of the decimal point. (RUN the program to make sure it works.)

4. Change the program to make the answer accurate to one decimal place. (For example, if R = 1, then Area (A) = 3.1.)

ABS(X) Function

- ABS(X) = Abbreviation for absolute value of X
- Examples:

  ABS (12) = 12   ABS (−10) = 10
  ABS (0) = 0   ABS (−357) = 357

- Note! ABS (25 − 10) = ABS (10 − 25) = 15

Assignment 14-2 ABS(X)

YOUR ACTION	DISPLAY
1. Type and enter the program shown.	10 INPUT "TYPE ANY POSITIVE OR NEGATIVE #"; N 20 X = ABS (N) 30 PRINT "N", "X" 40 PRINT N,X
2. RUN the program several times using both positive and negative numbers.	
(Note that regardless of the number you input as N, the absolute value of X is the same number without the sign.)	

RND(X) Function

- RND(X) or random number function causes the computer to give you a "surprise" number.
    - It's as though the computer spins a wheel of chance.
    - It's like pulling a number out of a hat.
    - It's unpredictable!
- The random number function – general form
    Let N = INT (X * RND(1)) + 1
  Where N = The random number
    RND = Abbreviation for random
    X = Any number between 1 and 32767
- The general form for finding random numbers may seem a little complicated at first but it's not once you understand how to use it. All you need to do is just give "X" the value or number you wish to be the highest random number. When you run the program, you will have a number between 1 and X.
  Example:
  10 PRINT INT (4 * RND (1)) +1 (will give you a random number from 1 to 4 inclusive)
  20 PRINT INT (6 * RND (1)) +1 (will give you a random number from 1 to 6 inclusive)
  30 PRINT INT (10 * RND (1)) +1 (will give you a random number from 1 to 10 inclusive)
- Type, enter, and RUN the above program several times or until you understand how random numbers work.

Random Number — Program Example

YOUR ACTION	DISPLAY
1. Type and enter. (Line 5 allows you to enter "X" or the highest random number you want.)	5 INPUT "ENTER A NO. BETWEEN 1 AND 100"; X 10 FOR J = 1 to 10 20 PRINT INT (X * RND (1)) +1 30 NEXT J
2. Type RUN and press RETURN .	(SCREEN SHOULD HAVE TEN RANDOM NUMBERS BETWEEN 1 AND X.)
3. RUN program again to get the idea.	
4. Change Line 10 to read:	10 FOR J = 1 TO 100
5. RUN. (Get the idea?)	(SCREEN SHOULD HAVE ONE HUNDRED RANDOM NUMBERS BETWEEN 1 AND X.)

Coin Toss Program

ACTION AND REMARKS

1. **Type and enter program as shown:**

   (Line 20 initializes counters, sets H = T = 0.)

   (Line 40 starts next line at top of screen.)

   (Line 60 begins FOR-NEXT statement and runs it "N" times.)

   (Line 70 generates integers between 1 and 2.)

   (Line 80 tells the program to go to Line 90 if X = 1 = heads and to Line 100 if X = 2 = tails.)

   (Line 90, "heads" are counted.)

   (Line 100, "tails" are counted.)

   (Line 110 sends control back to Line 60 for "N" passes.)

DISPLAY

```
5 REM**COIN TOSS PROGRAM**
10 REM**H = HEADS, T = TAILS**
20 H = 0: T = 0: PRINT
30 INPUT "HOW MANY TIMES SHALL I FLIP THE COIN"; N
40 HOME
50 PRINT "I'M FLIPPING THE COIN... STANDBY"
60 FOR K = 1 TO N
70 X = INT (2 * RND (1))+1
80 ON X GOTO 90, 100
90 H = H + 1 :GOTO 110
100 T = T + 1
110 NEXT K
120 HOME
```

Coin Toss Program (Con't)

ACTION AND REMARKS

(Line 13Ø prints the headings.)

(Line 14Ø prints the values of H, T, and N.)

(Line 15Ø calculates and prints the percentage of heads, percentage of tails.)

(Line 16Ø provides spacing for better appearance.)

DISPLAY

```
13Ø PRINT "HEADS", "TAILS",
    "TOTFLIPS" : PRINT
14Ø PRINT H, T, N

15Ø PRINT 1ØØ*H/N; "%", 1ØØ*T/N; "%"

16Ø PRINT: PRINT: PRINT
```

Assignment 14-3 RND(X)

YOUR ACTION	DISPLAY
1. Type and enter the program as shown.	5 REM ** PICK A NUMBER GAME ** 10 HOME 20 X = INT (10 * RND (1)) +1 30 INPUT "ENTER A NUMBER BETWEEN 1 & 10"; N 40 IF X = N THEN 100 50 IF X < N THEN 110 60 IF X > N THEN 120 100 PRINT "RIGHT ON": GOTO 10 105 FOR J = 1 TO 2500: NEXT: GOTO 10 110 PRINT "LOWER" : GOTO 30 120 PRINT "HIGHER" : GOTO 30
2. RUN the program.	

Assignment 14-3 RND(X)

3. Analyze the program.

    Line 10 _____ the display.

    Line 20 is the _____ generator.

    Line 30 allows the user to _____ a number.

    Lines 40, 50, and 60 are _____ statements that compare
                                                  conditional, unconditional

    the random number _____ with the input number _____.
                                X,N   X,N

    Lines 100, 110, and 120 are PRINT statements that guide the player.
    Why does Line 105 GOTO Line 10 and why do Lines 110 and 120 GOTO
    Line 30? Explain the function of Line 105.

4. Modify (change) the program to pick a number between 1 and 100, and RUN
   this program several times.

Summary

- **ABS(X)** — Provides the absolute value of X regardless of the number you input (i.e., X is that same number without the sign).
- **INT(X)** — Provides integer or whole number value of X.
    - If X is a positive (+) number, it chops off the decimal part.
    - If X is a negative number, it rounds down to the next lowest whole number (e.g., INT (−0.6) = −1).
- **RND(X)** — Causes the computer to give you a random number.
    - INT (X * RND (1)) + 1 gives you a random number from 1 to X inclusive.

PRACTICE 24

INT(X) and ABS(X)

1. Fill in the banks with the appropriate INT(X):

X	INT(X)
0.7	_____
−2.5	_____
6.365	_____
−0.8	_____
−10.65	_____
0	_____
3.2425	_____
−7.61	_____
−0.3	_____
0.3	_____

2. The following program can be used for finding the area of a circle:
   ```
   10 REM *** AREA OF A CIRCLE = 3.14159 * R ∧ 2 ***
   20 INPUT "THE RADIUS IS"; R
   25 INPUT "THE RADIUS IS IN (IN.,FT,OR YD,)"; A$
   30 A = 3.14159 * R ∧ 2
   40 PRINT "THE AREA IS "; A; " SQ. "; A$
   ```
   a. Enter and RUN the program several times to make certain it works.
   b. Change the program to suppress (chop off) all the numbers to the right of the decimal point (RUN the program to make sure it works).
   c. Change the program to make the answer accurate to one decimal place. (For example if R = 1, then area (A) = 3.1).

PRACTICE 25

Random Number

1. Write a program that will let you pick a random number between 1 and 100. The program should let you input a number from the keyboard and provide the following clues on your guess.
   a. If the number you pick matches the number the computer picks, have the computer PRINT "Right On."
   b. If the number from the keyboard is too high, have the program print "Lower."
   c. If the number from the keyboard is too low, have the program print "Higher."
   d. Enter and RUN the program several times.

PART 15

Subroutines

What You Will Learn

1. To explain the purpose for using subroutines.

2. To explain the purpose and use of terms ON-GOTO, GOSUB, RETURN, ON GOSUB.

3. To develop, enter, and run programs using subroutines and ON-GOTO statements.

Subroutine

What Is It?
- A subroutine is a short program or routine that is built into a large program to do specific calculations or perform repetitive functions.

Why Use It?
- There are times when you need the same type of calculation at various points in your program, but instead of retyping the statements needed for this calculation each time, you can write a subroutine to perform the needed calculations.

How Do You Call a Subroutine?
- To call or branch to a subroutine, use the GOSUB statement.
  - The GOSUB XXXXX statement directs the computer to go to that line number and execute the program steps until it reaches the key word RETURN, which ends the subroutine.
  - RETURN is always built into a subroutine and is used to tell the computer that the subroutine is finished. When finished, the control of the program is returned to the statement in the main program immediately following the most recently executed GOSUB.

Subroutine Example

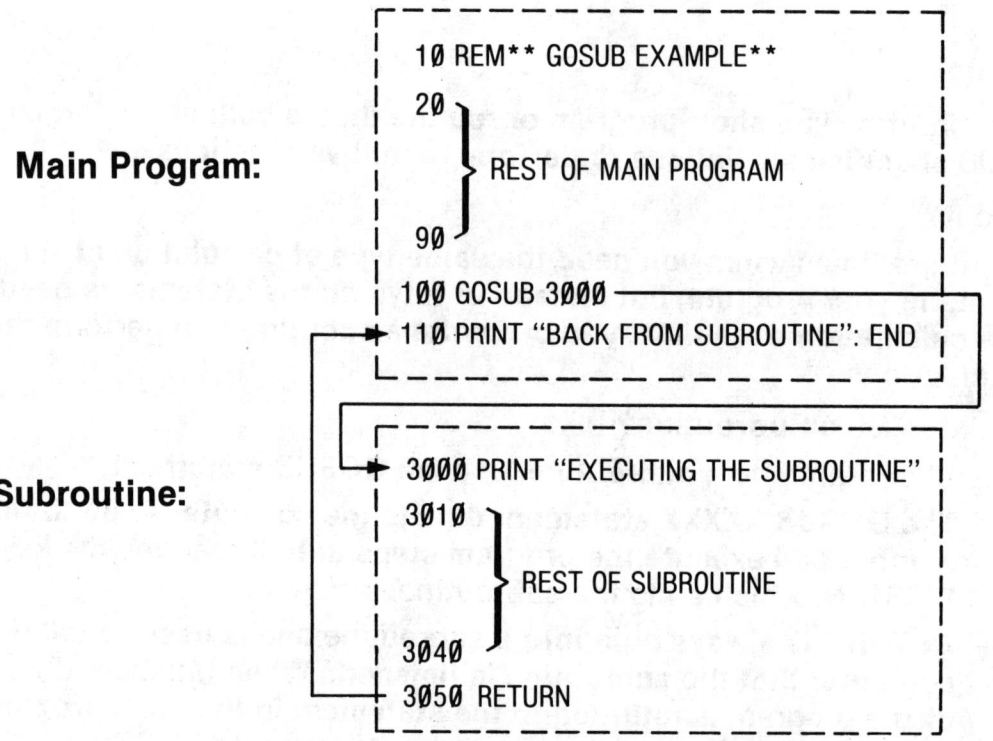

Subroutine Illustration

Main Program

```
10 REM** MAIN PROGRAM BEGINS HERE**
 •  _____
 •  _____
 •  _____
 •  _____
100 GOSUB 1000
110 REM**MAIN PROGRAM CONTINUES**
 •  _____
 •  _____
 •  _____
 •  _____
 •  _____
 •  _____
200 GOSUB 2000
210 REM**MAIN PROGRAM CONTINUES**
 •  _____
 •  _____
 •  _____
 •  _____
290 END REM*MAIN PROGRAM ENDS*
```

Subroutines

```
1000 REM*SUBROUTINE #1*
 •  _____
 •  _____
 •  _____
 •  _____
1060 RETURN


2000 REM*SUBROUTINE #2**
 •  _____
 •  _____
 •  _____
 •  _____
2050 RETURN
```

Subroutine Illustration (Con't)

1. When the computer reaches the GOSUB in Line 100, the program will branch (GOTO) Line 1000, which is the beginning of Subroutine #1.

2. After Subroutine #1 is executed and the RETURN (Line 1060) is reached, control is passed back to the main program (Line 110). Note that Line 110 is the next higher number after the GOSUB that put it in the subroutine (Line 100).

3. The computer continues through the main program to the GOSUB in Line 200, which branches control to Subroutine #2 in Line 2000.

4. After the subroutine is executed, the RETURN (Line 2050) passes the control back to Line 210 in the main program. (Note again that this is the next higher line number after the GOSUB in Line 200.)

5. An END statement is included in the program (Line 290) after the main program is finished to keep it from accidentally falling into the subroutine. We only want the subroutines to be executed when we call for them by a GOSUB.

Sample Program Using Subroutines
(Temperature Conversion)

Main Program
```
10 REM*TEMPERATURE CONVERSION PROGRAM**
15 HOME
20 INPUT "DO YOU WISH TO CONVERT C TO F (Y OR N)"; A$
30 IF A$ = "Y" THEN 80
40 PRINT: INPUT "DEGREES FAHRENHEIT"; F
50 GOSUB 2000
60 PRINT: INPUT "HAVE YOU FINISHED (Y OR N)"; B$
70 IF B$ = "N" THEN 40
75 END
80 PRINT: INPUT "DEGREES CENTIGRADE"; C
90 GOSUB 1000
100 PRINT: INPUT "HAVE YOU FINISHED (Y OR N)"; C$
110 IF C$ = "N" THEN 80
120 END
```

Subroutine #1
```
1000 REM**CELSIUS TO FAHRENHEIT CONVERSION**
1010 F = (9/5)* C + 32 : PRINT
1020 PRINT C; "DEGREES CELSIUS ="; F; "DEGREES FAHRENHEIT"
1030 RETURN
```

Subroutine #2
```
2000 REM**FAHRENHEIT TO CELSIUS CONVERSION**
2010 C = (F-32) * (5/9): PRINT
2020  PRINT F; "DEGREES FAHRENHEIT ="; C; "DEGREES CELSIUS"
2030 RETURN
```

Analysis of Sample Program Using Subroutines

1. Lines 10 through 110 comprise the main program.
2. Line 20 is an input statement to ask the user if he wants to convert from C to F or from F to C. Yes (Y) means C to F and No (N) means F to C.
3. Line 30 is a conditional branch statement. If the user wants to convert Centigrade C to Fahrenheit, then branch to Line 80; otherwise, skip a line (PRINT) and go to Line 40.
4. Line 40 allows the user to input the °F to be converted to °C.
5. Lines 50 and 90 call the subroutines.
6. Line 60 asks the user if he is finished. In Line 70 the program will branch to Line 40 (if B$ = N) or the program will END (if B$ ≠ N).
7. Line 80 is similar to Line 40, except that it allows the user to input the °C to be converted to °F.
8. Lines 100 and 110 are the same as Lines 60 and 70.
9. The first subroutine begins at Line 1000 and ENDS at Line 1030. It RETURNS control to Line 100 in the main program.
10. The second subroutine begins at Line 2000 and ENDS at Line 2030. It RETURNS control to Line 60 in the main program.

Subroutine Exercise

```
10 PRINT "THIS IS"; "   ";
20 GOSUB 1000
30 PRINT "OF HOW"; "  ";
40 GOSUB 2000
50 PRINT "WORKS"
60 END
1000 PRINT "AN EXAMPLE"; "  ";
1010 RETURN
2000 PRINT "A SUBROUTINE"; "  ";
2010 RETURN
```

1. Analyze the program and write the message. _____
2. Now type and enter the program.
3. RUN the program. Does it agree with your message?

Assignment 15-1

1. Analyze the program below and write the message:

```
10 LET B = 10
20 GOSUB 2000
30 B = B + 5
40 GOSUB 2000
50 B = B + 10
60 GOSUB 2000
99 END
2000 REM SUBROUTINE
2010 IF B<12 THEN 2050
2020 IF B = 25 THEN 2070
2030 PRINT "PRIME"
2040 GOTO 2080
2050 HOME: PRINT "LEEDS"
2060 GOTO 2080
2070 PRINT "COMPUTERS"
2080 RETURN
```

Message _____

ON-GOTO Example

YOUR ACTION

1. Type NEW and enter this program.

2. Before you RUN the program, analyze it. Can you predict what will happen when you RUN it? (I sure hope you can by now!)

3. RUN the program several times until you feel comfortable with it.

DISPLAY

```
5 HOME
10 INPUT "TYPE A NUMBER FROM 1 TO 3"; N
20 IF N = 1 THEN 110
30 IF N = 2 THEN 130
40 IF N = 3 THEN 150
50 PRINT "HEY, I WANT A NUMBER FROM 1 TO 3!"
60 GOTO 10
99 END
110 PRINT "N = 1"
120 END
130 PRINT "N = 2"
140 END
150 PRINT "N = 3"
160 END
```

ON-GOTO Example (Con't)

YOUR ACTION

DISPLAY

4. Erase Lines 20, 30, and 40. (Remember, there are two ways to do this! Use DEL or simply type in each line number separately and then press RETURN.

5. Type and enter this line:

6. List your program.

```
20 ON N GOTO 110, 130, 150
```
(SHOULD HAVE NEW LINE 20 + LINES 5, 10, AND 50 THROUGH 160 FROM PREVIOUS PAGE. IF YOU DON'T HAVE THESE LINES, FIX IT!)

7. RUN the program a few times.

(WORKS JUST THE SAME AS BEFORE, DOESN'T IT?)

8. RUN the program again. Use the following inputs:
   1.5
   1.8
   2.8
   0.8
   3.99

(Now do you understand that N = INT (N) or whole number?)

N = 1
N = 1
N = 2
HEY, I WANT A NUMBER BETWEEN 1 & 3!
N = 3

ON-GOTO Example Analysis

1. **Line 20 tells the computer to do the following:**
   - If, the integer (whole number) value of N is 1, GOTO Line 110.
   - If the integer value of N is 2, GOTO Line 120.
   - If the integer value of N is 3, GOTO Line 130.
   - If the integer value of N is not one of the numbers listed above, then move on to the next line.

2. **The ON-GOTO statement has a built-in INT statement, which really acts like this:**
   20 ON INT (N) GOTO----ETC.

Assignment 15-2 ON-GOTO

1. Type and enter the following program:
   ```
    5 HOME
   10 INPUT "ENTER A NUMBER FROM 1 TO 5"; N
   20 ON N GOTO 100, 200, 300, 400, 500
   30 PRINT "HEY I WANT A NUMBER FROM 1 TO 5!" : GOTO 10
   40 END
   100 PRINT "N = 1" : END
   200 PRINT "N = 2" : END
   300 PRINT "N = 3" : END
   400 PRINT "N = 4" : END
   500 PRINT "N = 5" : END
   ```

2. Answer the following questions before running the program
   a. What happens (output) if the input is 1.8 (Line 10)?_____
   b. What happens (output) if the input is 3.99? _____
   c. What happens (output) if the input is 2.89? _____
   d. What happens if the input is 0.5? _____

3. RUN the program several times and record the following:

   INPUT   OUTPUT

ON-GOSUB

- Works like ON-GOTO, except control branches to one of the subroutines specified by the line numbers in the line number list.
- Example:
  ```
  10 INPUT "CHOOSE 1, 2, OR 3"; K
  20 ON K GOSUB 1000, 2000, 3000
  99 END
  1000 PRINT "SUBROUTINE #1" : RETURN
  2000 PRINT "SUBROUTINE #2" : RETURN
  3000 PRINT "SUBROUTINE #3" : RETURN
  ```
- K may be a numerical constant, variable, or expression.
  — It must have a positive value, however, or an error will occur.
- If K ≠ 1, 2, or 3, the program will go to the next line (99 END).

Summary

- GOSUB XXXX, causes the computer to:
  — Go to the subroutine beginning at line XXXX (the specified line number).
  — Work through the subroutine until it finds a RETURN statement.
  — Return control to the statement that follows the GOSUB statement in the main program.

- ON n GOSUB XXXX, ······, YYYY
  — Multi-way branching statement that is controlled by a test variable (n), which sends control of the program to one of the subroutines specified by line numbers in the line number list (i. e., XXXX,····, YYYY).
  — The test variable n must be a numerical constant, variable, or expression that has a non-negative value or else an error will occur.

- ON n GOTO XXXX, ····, YYYY
  — Works like ON n GOSUB except control branches to one of the line numbers specified (XXXX, ····, YYYY).
  — ON n GOTO 1st line number, 2nd line number ——— nth line number expression must be between 0 and 255 inclusive.
  — If n<0, an error will occur.

PRACTICE 26

Program to Convert Centigrade to Fahrenheit and Vice Versa

1. Write a program that will do the following:
   a. Convert Centigrade to Fahrenheit.
   b. Convert Fahrenheit to Centigrade.
   c. Allow you to select either A or B above.
   d. Allow you to input from keyboard.
   e. PRINT the answer as follows:

   - ___*___ degrees Celsius = ___**___ degrees Fahrenheit

     or

     ___*___ degrees Fahrenheit = ___**___ degrees Celsius

   * Keyboard input value
   ** Calculated output value

PRACTICE 27

Program for Sample Profit/Loss Statement

1. When a product is sold for more than it costs, the seller receives a profit. When a product is sold for less than it costs, the seller takes a loss.

   Therefore: sell price − cost = profit or loss

   If we let: S = Sell price
   C = Cost
   U = No. of units
   P = Profit
   L = Loss
   Then: P (or L) = S*U − C*U

   a. Write a program that will compute the profit or loss for a business if the sell price and cost are known. (*Note:* Program should permit you to enter cost and sell price from the keyboard.)
   b. Have the computer PRINT the following:

NO. OF UNITS	_____
UNIT PRICE ($)	_____
UNIT COST ($)	_____
TOTAL SALES ($)	_____
TOTAL COST ($)	_____
PROFIT/LOSS ($)	_____
% OF SALES	_____

   c. RUN the program several times and record your answer.

EXTRA PRACTICE 1

Programming Mathematical Operators

1. Given two numbers A=25 and B=5:
    a. Write one program that will add, subtract, divide (A/B), multiply, and square the two numbers (A and B).
    b. The answer should PRINT as shown here:
       The sum of A and B is _____ (your answer).
       The difference of A and B is _____ (your answer).
       The quotient of (A/B) is _____ (your answer).
       The product of A*B is _____ (your answer).
       The square of A is _____ (your answer).
       The square of B is _____ (your answer).

EXTRA PRACTICE 2

Finding the Average

1. Write a progam to find the average of three numbers.
2. Have the program PRINT: The average is _____.
3. Add a program line to have the program PRINT the average of your # _____, your # _____, and your # _____ is your answer _____. Example: The average of 3, 4, and 8 is 5.

EXTRA PRACTICE 3

More Mathematical Operations

Write five separate programs to PRINT the answer to these problems (the answer should read 25 * 2 + 4 = 54, and so on.):

1. 25*2+4
2. $3^2 + 4 - 2$
3. 36 ÷ 4 *5
4. 28 + 4 * 6 ÷ 8
5. (18−2) ÷ 3 + 4 (6*3) + 2^3

EXTRA PRACTICE 4

Print Zones

Part I.

Write a program to PRINT the word "Leeds" in the following ways:

	ZONE 1	ZONE 2	ZONE 3
1.	LEEDS	LEEDS	LEEDS
2.	LEEDS		LEEDS
3.		LEEDS	
4.		LEEDS	LEEDS
5.			LEEDS

Part II.

Using page 77, type in the information as shown (]MICROCOMPUTERS*)...and so on.
1. Count the number of characters in all three zones. How many?
2. How many in zone 1 _____, zone 3, _____.

EXTRA PRACTICE 5

Area of Square and Volume of Cube

1. Write a program to solve the following problems. Label your answers.
    a. The side of a square is 27 inches. Find its area (area (A) = s^2).
    b. If the side of a cube is also 27 inches, find its volume (volume (V) = s^3).
2. Using INPUT statements, write a program to find the area of a square and volume of a cube.
    a. Solve the problems above (assume sides of square and cube are equal).
    b. Using different lengths for the side, RUN the program again (assume that the sides of the square and the cube are equal).

EXTRA PRACTICE 6

Printing Tables of Numbers, Squares, and Cubes

1. Write a program to generate the first 25 numbers and PRINT their squares on the same line.
    Example: 1   1
               2   4
               3   9
               4   16
    and so forth
2. Write a program to generate the first 25 numbers and PRINT their cubes on the same line.
    Example: 1   1
               2   8
               3   27
               4   64
    and so forth
3. Write a program to generate all the numbers from 20 to 1 and PRINT the numbers, and their squares and cubes, on the same line and in four columns.
    Example: 20   400   8000   160000
               19   361   6859   130321
               18   324   5832   104976
    and so forth

EXTRA PRACTICE 7

Printing Three Times and Nine Times Tables

1. Write a program to generate the three times table from $3 \times 1 = 3$ to $3 \times 12 = 36$. The printout should look exactly like this:
              3 * 1 = 3
              3 * 2 = 6
              3 * 3 = 9
              3 * 4 = 12
    and so forth
2. Write a program to generate the nine times table from $9 \times 1 = 9$ to $9 \times 12 = 108$.

EXTRA PRACTICE 8

Two-Dimensional Array

1. Suppose we have a class of ten students. The course grade is based upon three quizzes, and the results for the class are as follows:

Student #	1	2	3	4	5	6	7	8	9	10
Quiz #										
1	88	41	100	88	79	76	86	90	85	100
2	75	52	65	57	98	86	96	91	86	92
3	71	47	75	77	86	96	85	92	97	82

   a. Write a program to PRINT the following information:

Student #	Course Avg./Student	
1	?	
2	?	Computer calculates
3	?	and PRINTS average
4	?	

and so forth

Quiz #	Class Avg./Quiz	
1	?	
2	?	Computer calculates
3	?	and PRINTS average